The
London B-Type
Motor Omnibus

WORLD OF TRANSPORT

THE LONDON B-TYPE MOTOR OMNIBUS
Third and Revised Edition
The story of the world's first major standardised motor bus
fleet, operated by the London General Omnibus Company between
1910 and 1927, including the sale to other operators both in
Great Britain and overseas. Also its use during the First
World War, 1914 - 1918 in France and on the home front.

G. J. Robbins and J. B. Atkinson. © 1991

Published by D.P.R. Marketing and Sales (The World of Transport)
37 Heath Road, Twickenham, Middlesex TW1 4AW England.
ISBN 1 - 871979 - 04 - 8

Front Cover.
A busy scene in London around 1914/15. painted by Pete Insole.
© DPR Marketing and Sales. 1991

Photographic credits

London Transport	Page nos viii, 17, 24, 43, 48
Imperial War Museum	Page nos 52, 113.
Late E. G. Masterman	Page nos 81, 89, 94.
Mrs Hinton	Page no 114.
J. B. Atkinson	Page no 114.
J. C. Gillham	Page no 115.

All others are from the G. Robbins collection.

D.T.P by Keyless, Headley Down, Hampshire , England.
Printed and Bound by Biddles Limited,
Guildford and Kings Lynn, England.

CONTENTS

PETER INSOLE

The front cover art work was commissioned by DPR Marketing and Sales after seeing one of Pete's prints. We trust that you feel that he has captured the B-Type Motor Omnibus in all its splendour, in the period 1914/1915.

Pete has exhibited at the Royal Academy and is concentrating his efforts on his first love of painting buses, trams and trains

If you have a favourite transport subject and you would like to commission Pete Insole. Send full details and as much information about the backgroud you require in the picture to Pete Insole, Dept B, 26 Primrose Hill, Haverhill, Diss, Suffolk CB9 9LS. Prices start at around £150.00, but ask for a quotation and delivery time.

We feel sure that this artists work will appreciate in value in the the years to come.

FOREWORD

J. B. Atkinson

I grew up with this bus. Every early adventure somehow began with it and as the years of boyhood spell the unforgettable dawn of freedom, so the great ungainly red rumbling friendly open-topped B-type has had a fascination for me as long as I can remember. To a five-year old boy they were far the most colourful and exciting objects on the streets of Wartime Kensington, and the evocative names on the boards they bore could be read aloud with delight. At seven I was riding the buses up Holland Park Avenue daily to school. At eight I stood on the front of the top deck when the maroons went off to signal the end of the Great War and the crowd around me went mad; someone lifted me over the front and on to the driver's roof or I would have been crushed.

At ten it was the B-type bus which took me seated high above the hedgerows to holidays in the country as far afield as Welwyn or Dorking and at twelve all over Town in long, lone, delightful explorations such as any boy can know, penetrating as far over London as sixpence pocket money would go in half-fares - and that was a long way in those days. And when living in Hammersmith, I was sent to school at Islington my range was vastly broadened.

Any Londoner will appreciate the exciting variety of routes there were for getting from one to another. In addition to being my friendly chariots of adventure, the buses became an absorbing interest and a hobby and I haunted Hammersmith garage, took notes of bus numbers and made a large and handsome model of B 7 that I wish I still possessed.

A few privileged occasions - after 1921 - when I was taken round Chiswick Works were treats never to be forgotten. On such visits, however, the main interest for me was the B-type, and I would walk along the assembly line (it was called a rope way then) from the point where a crane listed a bare frame from a pile and put it on trestles to the point at the end where the shining rebuilt chassis received its bonnet cover and eventually fitted with the next overhauled body from store.

FOREWORD
G. J. Robbins

I too grew up with the B-type bus and my earliest recollections are of the single-deck buses on route 111 passing the house where we lived in Stroud Green Road in 1916. One day one of these single-deckers broke down and later caught fire. In the later war years we lived at Westerham and I only saw an occasional East Surrey bus and it was not until 1919 that I saw the B-type again at Dulwich when they replaced Tillings on the 78 route and the National Steam Car buses on 12A. These were all Traffic Emergency buses, most in khaki but others in red. I noted the variety of bodies on these buses particularly some with a strange white canopy over the driver's cab which I found later had come off the Great Eastern Y-type vehicles. Although I soon became familiar with the Metropolitan fleet name I was surprised to see some with Associated, Gearless and Southern names. Taking notes of bus numbers I found that most B-type had numbers below B 2700 but there were many between B4900 and 5100 and stranger still some as high as B 6865 - 6889. It was in 1921 that I again saw single deck B-type buses which were the 26-seaters and had appeared one day at Forest Hill on the 109 to Chislehurst. I was therefore very pleased when Mr Atkinson asked me to work with him on this book.

This book has been made possible to some extent by the metriculous records kept by the late Percy J. Fyson who carefully noted the registration numbers and first garages of all the B-type buses that he saw from 1912 onwards. We have also been helped by access to many official records for which we are most grateful.

A typical London General horse bus that would eventually be replaced by a B-type motor bus. It is seen in Tottenham Court Road when working on the Victoria and Kings Cross service. Its running letters are MFD.

The B-type arrives! A busy scene outside the Mansion House late in 1910. B40 on route 8 and another on the 25 are seen in the foreground.

Regent Street 1913, B-type buses on routes 51A. 12 and 20 proceeding southwards whilst opposite is a M.E.T. Daimler followed by a National Steam Car and a Tilling on route 12.

CHAPTER 1

PREPARING THE WAY FOR THE NEW BUS
G. J. Robbins

In order that the reader may have an idea of the ancestry of the B-type motor bus of the London General Omnibus Company and the events leading up to its introduction in the year 1910, the following notes are supplied.

London's road transport in the nineteenth century was dominated by the horse. Only a few experiments in mechanical traction had taken place in the closing years of the century and none of them had had any great success. By the early 1850's there was intense competition between the horse buses in London which led to crawling or racing buses and road congestion. This competition increased during the time of the Great Exhibition of 1851. Similar problems had occurred in Paris, which had been the birthplace of the bus as a service of sorts had operated there in 1662. In July 1854 a monopoly was granted for the running of the whole of Paris horse bus services and the Paris Bus Company was formed. This led to a proposal for a similar unified service in London by amalgamating the existing bus proprietors. Accordingly, in 1855 a company was formed in Paris (with an authorised capital of £1 million) to become known as the Compagnie Générale de Londres with head office in Paris and a London office at 454 West Strand. The co-operation of four of the established bus proprietors in London was obtained who arranged for the buying up of 'times' vehicles and equipment. 'Times' was the method of determining the number of buses on routes which at that time was governed by Associations which provided that all buses on a route were painted in the same colours although run by various operators. Although the new company was French in origin, for all practical purposes it was a British concern and the French title was discontinued on 11th January 1856 in favour of 'London General Omnibus Company'. At the outset it had owned some six hundred buses, about two thirds of the total in London, at that time. Over the years the horse bus improved, but only gradually, developing from a small single-deck vehicle to a double-decker seating twelve passengers inside on longitudinal seats and fourteen on top facing forward on garden seats, this style having been first produced about 1882. The early motor bus was to some extent based on this type of horse bus.

There was considerable competition among the various horse bus companies, and this intensified in 1881 with the formation of the London Road Car Company. The proprietors chose this title to avoid the use of the hated term 'omnibus' which was considered foreign and to emphasize its British origin adopted the fleet name 'Union Jack'. It made good progress and at the turn of the century had a fleet of

The London B-Type Motor Omnibus

480 out of a total licensed in London of 3,736.

The L.G.O.C. had the largest fleet but another competitor was Thomas Tilling running mainly in the South of London.

During the early years of the twentieth century all three companies experimented with motor buses, but few of these continued in service for any length of time. By the middle of 1905 the 'General' had only four motor buses, 'Road Car' had nineteen, while a newly formed company, the London Motor Omnibus Company had sixteen and Thomas Tilling twelve. The Milnes-Daimler was the most popular make, featuring mainly in the fleets of the last two companies mentioned.

The L.G.O.C. had reached its maximum fleet of horse buses in operation in 1905 when its total was 1,418. and 7,000 horses. The early motor buses were very temperamental and had many breakdowns, so that horsed transport was still holding its own. Nevertheless the new form of traction was improving all the time and more motor buses were put into service by the main companies as well as by a number of smaller operators.

The London Motor Omnibus Company which had no horse bus 'roots' commenced on March 27 1905 when five Milnes Daimlers were put on a route between Brondesbury and Law Courts. The Company which adopted the fleet name 'Vanguard' had a fleet of 58 buses by the end of the year. Three subsidiary companies were introduced, first, the London & District Motor Bus Company on August 30 1905, followed soon by London and Provincial Motor Bus Company both using the fleet name 'Arrow'. The third subsidiary was Motor Bus Company which ran a number of buses under the fleet name 'Pilot' from July 31 1906. All three were absorbed by the Vanguard on April 1 1907, bringing the Vanguard total of buses up to 310. Most were Milnes Daimlers which had proved most satisfactory although later a number of De Dions were obtained. Other types had been tried but soon withdrawn the bodies and registrations numbers transferred to Milnes Daimlers. Vanguards most ambitious venture was a daily service between London and Brighton the inaugural run being made on August 30 1905. This came to an unfortunate stop following the disastrous Handcross Hill accident when a Vanguard Milnes Daimler on Private Hire overturned on July 12 1906. Vanguard buses worked from a garage at Albany Street near Regents Park, and later had garages at Old Kent Road and Shepherds Bush as well as Dalston at first used by Pilot. Vanguard also acquired a factory in Blackhorse Road, Walthamstow where engineering work on their buses took place and new buses were obtained by assembling parts manufactured by other firms. Ten such buses were built late in 1906 these being known as M.O.C. (Motor Omnibus Construction). Vanguard used no fleet numbers but relied on registration numbers for identification, and to commence with obtained a batch of numbers A9101-9200 followed by LC 5001-5100 and LN 301-400. The ex-Arrow buses were numbered LC 2200-49 and a further set from LC 3800. The former Pilot numbers were in the series LC 7300-99. Vanguard also obtained registration numbers LN 5975-99 for lorries in a Haulage Department. Many of these numbers were later to be found on B-type buses. It was in 1906 that Vanguard gave numbers to their bus routes and numbers 1 to 10 were soon operating in London followed by 11 and 12. Many of these routes were to continue up to the present time.

By 1905 the London Road Car Company had over 500 pair-horsed buses with

2

nearly 5,000 horses. They had introduced four experimental motor buses late in 1904 and 32 were put into service during 1905. Many of these early motor buses were of German manufacture including 12 Germains and 24 Durkopps none of which continued long in service. A similar number of Clarkson steam buses were obtained but all withdrawn early in 1907. The company found the Straker Squire buses most suitable and eventually ran some 215 of this make. The Union Jack garages were at Farm Lane in Fulham also at Putney, Battersea and Upton Park. Following the lead set by Vanguard the Road Car Company obtained registration numbers, LC 2300-49, LC 4100-99, LN 200-99 and LN 7100-25.

The first motor bus of the London General Omnibus Company was a small single deck Clarkson steam bus introduced in October 1904 followed by a small double deck Orion. It was May 1905 before a more suitable double deck LGOC bus appeared in the form of a Milnes Daimler and twenty motor buses were operated by the end of 1905. Experiments were made with several different makes including twelve Clarkson steam buses. De Dions were found to be one most reliable, and LC 918, a De Dion new in December 1905 was the first bus to carry the fleet name General. It was a Cricklewood garage bus with 'times' letters EH-R. Eventually 100 Wolseleys were ordered and they came into service from February 1907 but a number of General's new buses had been refused licensing by the Metropolitan Police on account of their weight. LGOC opened a garage at Cricklewood to house these early buses and as the fleet grew another was obtained at Acton followed in 1906 by Mortlake and later by Athol Street at Poplar, where many of the Wolseleys were sent as they arrived. The General was very keen on numbers which were given to both chassis and bodies. Body numbers started at 1 for the early motor bus bodies and this system continued throughout the years. From 1906 numbers appeared on the buses in the form of a fleet number and the various makes were classified as follows, from 1 upwards for Bussings, 01 for Milnes Daimlers 100 upwards for Straker Squires, 200 for De Dions, 400 for Clarksons Steam, and 500 up for Wolseleys. General like the other companies obtained batches of registration numbers LC 3700-99, LC 8600-99, and lastly LN 4500-99. A feature on all LGOC motor buses from the first one was the display of the 'times' or 'running' letters shown at the top of the side windows alongside the driver. From 1910 these were moved to the bottom of these side windows. They consisted of three letters for example the first Bussing had letters EH-A, the 'E' indicated the garage, Cricklewood, 'H' the route, Cricklewood and Law Courts and 'A' being the first bus on the route. In February 1906 nine buses from Cricklewood were transferred to Acton garage and were re-lettered AH-A to AH-I. These letters were a continuation of a similar system used for the horse buses and then the first letter represented the area that the horse buses were stabled, and as the motor bus garages were opened they acquired the letter of the horse bus area thus 'E' and 'A' in the examples given. When regular bus routes became established the running letters were further developed and each route had two letters the first being for early duties and the second for later duties. The Cricklewood - Victoria route was EH-A for early buses and EI-A for later buses. The crews stayed with the buses having early turns one week and later turns the next. This system continued until December 1911.

There was considerable increase in the number of motor buses in London during 1907, a total of 933 being licenced at the end of that year, 802 of these were owned

A 26 an early Vanguard Milnes Daimler which passed to General in 1908 is seen when working on the 17 route, Ealing and East Ham in 1911

by the three large companies. This led to severe competition also these companies, Vanguard, Road Car and LGOC were in financial difficulty so that early in 1908 proposals were put forward towards some form of amalgamation. Eventually on July 1, 1908 the LGOC absorbed both Vanguard and London Road Car, adding respectively 386 and 225 buses to its own fleet of 288, although it still owned a number of horse buses. The motor buses of the three companies continued to be licensed separately until the end of 1908 and for a year or more vehicles still carried Vanguard or Union Jack fleet names. This amalgamation provided the LGOC with the valuable overhaul works at Walthamstow as well as the haulage and hire business from Vanguard. In August 1908 the LGOC system of 'times' letters were extended to Vanguard and Road Car as their garages were allocated code letters in the various areas in which they were situated. Then on October 1 1908 General and Road Car routes were numbered in an extension of the Vanguard system the result being 20 London bus services. Early in 1909 a method of numbering was introduced for all motor vehicles, type letters being allocated irrespective of original ownership. Types A, D and E, were Milnes Daimlers, General had a few A and D type but all the rest were ex Vanguard. F and G were Straker Squires. The F came from all three companies but the G were Road Car. H were Wolseleys ex General. J and P were Bussings ex General. K were M.O.C. and Armstrong Whitworth ex Vanguard. L, M and N were De Dion, L ex General, the M both General and Vanguard the N all Vanguard. Q were Thornycroft mainly lorries, R was given to six Road Car Maudslays, S was Generals Clarkson steam buses and T was allocated to a solitary Arrol Johnston from Vanguard. Following this renumbering there was

4

a redistribution of all the buses which were allocated to garages according to type. This may have taken place on March 3 1909 with the opening of the new bus garage at Norwood to which were sent the G type Straker Squires, most of which were still in Union Jack livery. The distribution is shown in the following list.

Garage	Total types	A	D/E	F	G	H	J	K	L	M	N	P	S	Q
Acton	36								36					
Albany St	65		65											
Athol St	63		63											
Battersea	88					88								
Old Kent Rd	55						7					48		
Cricklewood	69			69										
Farm Lane	36			36										
Felsham Rd	30									30				
Levan Rd	13												13	
Dalston	74		51								23			
Mortlake	78									78				
Normand Rd	50			50										
Upton Park	43	43												
Shepherds Bush	61		43					18						
Norwood	44				44									
	805	43	222	155	44	88	7	18	36	108	23	48	13	-
Private Hire Lorries/Vans unlicensed Buses	128	17	20	56	6	2	3	2	11	-	2	-	-	9
Total	933	60	242	211	50	90	10	20	47	108	25	48	13	9

The S type Clarkson Steamers were withdrawn in October 1909 the Levin Road garage at Poplar closed. Most of the other buses continued until gradually they were replaced by the, new B type.

Most of the bodies of the motor buses were of a similar pattern, with 32 or 34 seats - 16 longitudinally inside and 18 outside on "garden seats" copied from the horse buses. Normally these bodies were very strongly built and often outlasted the chassis on which they were mounted. However in certain instances a satisfactory bus could be extremely heavy which added to the difficulties, since on August 30 1909, the Commissioner of Police for the Metropolis issued new motor bus regulations, the main restrictions being in respect of weight and capacity; the maximum unladen weight was to be three and a half tons, or six tons loaded, with not more than four tons on the back axle. Seating was not to exceed 34 passengers referring of course to double-deckers; single-deckers were not considered at that time economic to operate.

When therefore after the amalgamation the Company was considering placing a large order for new buses, Colonel Frank Searle, their chief motor engineer, suggested that the Company should design and manufacture its own vehicles; it

M2 a General De Dion outside the 'Stapleton' in Stroud Green in 1911. The De Dions were
the most reliable of the early buses and the last to be replaced by B-type.

LC 7372 was the second X-type to enter service in December 1909. All the first eighteen
X-type were allocated to Fulham, Farm Lane garage for route 15.

All the X-type buses were allocated to the new gargae at Middle Row, North Kensington when it opened in May 1910 and most ran on route 7. X40 has been fitted with an experimental wire-netting guard.

already possessed an overhaul works at Walthamstow which it had inherited from 'Vanguard'. His suggestion was adopted, and the result was the design of a new type of bus designated X-type. The first of these was completed on August 12 1909, but some difficulty was experienced in securing a police licence, mainly on the grounds of the noise, which was particularly evident when magnified by solid-tyred vehicles running on the cobbled streets of the period. Eventually it was licensed and went into public service on December 16 1909.

Contemporary writers referred to it somewhat contemptuously as the "Daimler-Wolseley-Straker-type" and several years later Col. Searle himself wrote that "in the manufacture of the X-type we cribbed shamelessly. Any parts of the 28 types which had stood up to the gruelling of the London streets were embodied in it". Nevertheless the X-type was undoubtedly a praiseworthy achievement and moreover it was the prelude to the production of a far greater successor, the famous B-type.

A total of sixty X type buses were built plus one put to use as a garage lorry. X1 to X29 carried the registration numbers LC 7371-99 being the remainder of a batch inherited from Vanguard but originally issued to Pilot. X30 - 41 had registrations LN 4588-99 the balance of LGOC's batch numbers A new series from LN 9950 was obtained for the remaining X type continuing to LN 9969. Three X type were in service during December 1909, the next three not until March 1910 twelve more were licenced during April and May all eighteen went to Farm Lane garage at Fulham for route 15. A new bus garage was opened on May 12 1910 at Middle Row,

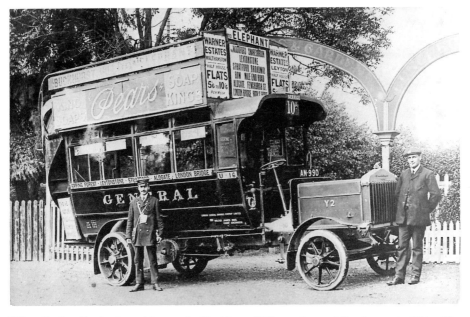

Y2, a Straker Squire is waiting at the Buckhurst Hill terminus of Sunday route 10A. The Y-type were formerly in the fleet of the Great Eastern Omnibus Company and many had this unsual curved canopy over the driver.

North Kensington and the X type were transferred to it from Farm Lane. All the rest of the X type order built between May and September 1910 went to Middle Row and operated on route 7. They had the standard 34-seat bodies built by LGOC at North Road Works. The X type were the first buses to have the route boards showing six lines of detail situated in the centre of the top deck with advertisements either side and this became standard on all new bodies for the B type.

Another bus company which had a sizeable fleet was the Great Eastern London Motor Omnibus Company Ltd., It was formed on March 22, 1906 to take over the motor bus services of a company that started life in 1888 as a horse tramway and later ran horse buses. Negotiations for a take over of this company by the LGOC had commenced in 1909 but it was not finally completed until April 1911 when LGOC took over the Great Eastern's 90 motor buses and three garages. These were at Lea Bridge Road, and Russell Road, Leyton, Green Street, Upton Park which General named Forest Gate and Lonsdale Road at Kilburn. Its four bus routes were Leyton and Elephant & Castle which was numbered 35, West Kilburn and Ilford and West Kilburn and Victoria 37 and 36 and Hackney and Putney combined with LGOC route 22. It had a fleet of 60 early Straker Squires which were included in the LGOC 'F' type, thirty Arrol Johnstons which joined the 'T' class and two of a later type of Straker Squire of which fifty were on order and these were given the type letter 'Y', the remainder of the order being delivered direct to the LGOC.

CHAPTER 2

DESIGN AND CONSTRUCTION OF THE NEW BUS
J. D. Atkinson

The design of the new bus, to be manufactured in large numbers by the London General Omnibus Company itself, was both light and sturdy for its time. It incorporated the best points in the design of many chassis which the Company had inherited or with which it had experimented, together with the experience gained from the running of the small fleet of X-type mentioned, in the last chapter. The design was begun in March 1910, and seven months later the first bus entered service the cost being some three hundred pounds, of which the body accounted for between one-third and one-half of the total.

The designers, Col. Frank Searle and Walter Iden, chose the best features of other designs, simplified them where possible, designed a new engine slightly smaller than that of the X-type, and improved the transmission line. They had to choose between chain and worm for final drive (both of which types were currently giving good service in the fleet), between wood and steel for frame and wheels, and between spur-gears and silent chain for the gearbox. They chose wooden frame, steel wheels, worm drive and chain gearbox, and this set the pattern for one of the most successful commercial vehicle chassis for the next twenty years.

The chassis frame was built, up of white ash with 5/32" flitch-plates of nickel steel on both sides of the wooden core. This extended to the full length of the frame, and there were cross-members of the same construction opposite the rear spring mountings and at points required to carry the various units, while the engine was carried in a steel sub-frame. A light tubular cross-member joined the dumb-irons and carried the starting handle.

The rear spring mountings were cast brackets enclosing the frame in a cradle and were riveted through it from the sides, while the front springs were anchored in steel dumbirons angled sharply downward from the frame into which they were recessed and riveted, the rear end of these springs having light shackles fitted to the underside of the frame and bolted vertically through the wood core.

There were variations to wheelbase through the years. The makers' chassis-lists show a figure of 12ft.10in. for buses up to B2822, 14ft. for B3474-B3503 (none of which carried double-deck bodies) and likewise for B4879-B4892 (which did have double-deck bodies but seem to have been unpopular with the licensing authorities - perhaps for their larger turning circle) and 13 ft. for most others. However altering the wheelbase was fairly easy, a matter of eight new holes through the frame and altering the length of the open propellor shaft, and the L.G.O.C. later did it themselves a good deal when converting chassis to 14ft. wheelbase to take large singledeck bodies. Frames were often to be seen in use with more than one set of holes for the rear spring mountings.

The track was 5ft. 8in. and the ground clearance at the lowest point (the tie-rod passing under the rear axle) was ten and a quarter inches. The wheels were of cast steel and varied both in design and in number of spokes. Front wheels might have six or seven circular spokes or eight flat ones with reinforcing ribs while rear wheels had either eight circular spokes or sixteen reinforced ribs combining to form eight at the hub. The latter type of rear wheel gradually replaced the earlier type, but both the seven and eight-spoked front wheels remained in use throughout. Tyres, which in earlier motor bus days had been prohibitively expensive, were by 1910 fairly reliable; from their extreme cost of ten pence per mile and a life of a few hundred miles in 1902, their cost was now down to twopence a mile on contract, with a life in tens of thousands of miles.

The front axle beam was an I-section stamping and the swivel axles carried plain floating bushes of phosphor-bronze on the hubs. The bushes had recessed oilways cut in them, enabling shorter hubs to be used than those of the X-type which had protruded excessively and, being out of the driver's sight, were often damaged. The rear wheels ran on floating bushes between hardened steel liners and had the steel brake-drums bolted directly on to the spokes, with internal expanding brake shoes and detachable linings. There was a contracting-band type of transmission brake on the short exposed drive-shaft between clutch and gearbox.

In later years, those buses intended for use on hilly routes (mostly single-deckers) were fitted with a simple sprag-gear to prevent running back.

The gearbox was of the silent-chain pattern with sliding dog-clutches, housed in a massive unit mounted almost half way along the chassis in order to distribute weight. It was connected to the clutch and to the rear axle by two splined shafts of almost equal length, having-heavy fabric universal joints except for the rear of the gearbox, where a steel-ball type was used. There were three forward speeds, with multiple-link silent chains, selected by a right-hand, gearlever in a "gate" with a small foot-pedal to protect reverse gear. The gear-lever and the large hand-brake lever were mounted outside the offside frame member. Power was transmitted through a large conical clutch with leather facings and held in engagement by a single central helical spring.

The engine was a four-cylinder side-valve unit of either 100mm. bore and 140mm. stroke, giving about 30 h.p. from 5.3 litres, or of 115mm. x 140mm. giving 36 h.p. from 5.7 litres. The larger engines were later often fitted with Ferodo single-plate clutches in place of the leather-faced type with a cone. The four cylinders were cast in pairs including the heads, which had screwed inspection caps for access to the valves, which were large (42mm. diameter) and almost immune from distortion. The sparking plugs were mounted on some models horizontally and on others in the more usual vertical position.

Ignition was by a magneto with a vernier coupling for setting. The pistons were made of cast iron with four rings. Lubrication was by pump to the four big-end troughs, but was otherwise by splash from the sump. The crankshaft was carried in three main bearings of bronze shells with white-metal linings.

The carburettor, of an up-draught lay-out was mounted low down on the near

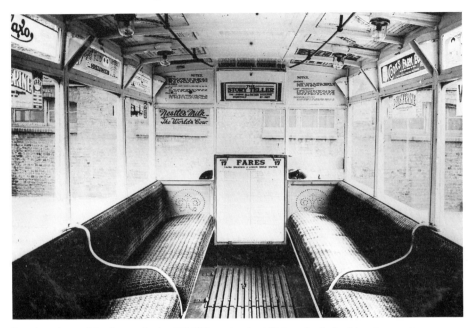

Interior view of the lower deck of B 770, a standard B-type body looking forward.

side of the engine with a long tube from the manifold, which made cold starting difficult but was considered necessary to ensure adequate gravity flow from the petrol tank, which was a 28-gallon one under the driver's seat. An external tap on the nearside frame was provided to cut off the flow in emergency. For cold starting a choke was fitted, and worked from the front by a wire loop accessible to the man swinging the starting handle, while for very cold weather the cylinders could be primed with raw petrol through the small brass taps on the cylinder heads.

Cooling was by thermo-syphon circulation though many later engines had water pumps. There was a by-pass through the waterjacket to warm the induction pipe, and the radiator had a small belt-driven fan. The first radiators had plain copper tubes, but later ones had gilled tubes in five offset banks. The earlier radiators were flat-topped with the letters "LGOC" cast in the header-tank, but from about 1914 there was an alternative design, similar in outline to that of Daimler with a larger header-tank rising in an elegant curve to the filler-cap and carrying the word 'General' in the ring-and-bar symbol.

The engine developed about 25 h.p. at its optimum speed of 800 r.p.m. (on later models about 30 h.p.at 1,000 r.p.m.) and had excellent torque characteristics due, to the long stroke and large flywheel. The rear axle ratio of 7.33 to 1 gave a top-gear speed of about 16 m.p.h. at 1,000 r.p.m. This was already above the then legal speed limit of twelve miles an hour and as this engine performed smoothly up to at least 2,000 r.p.m. speeds of 30 to 35 m.p.h. were sometimes attained. Towards the end of their life, when pairs of these buses were sometimes used, if highly unofficially and improperly, as what came to be "shadow buses" to harass the early

The London B-Type Motor Omnibus

GENERAL ARRANGEMENT OF STANDARD DOUBLE-DECK OMNIBUS BODY

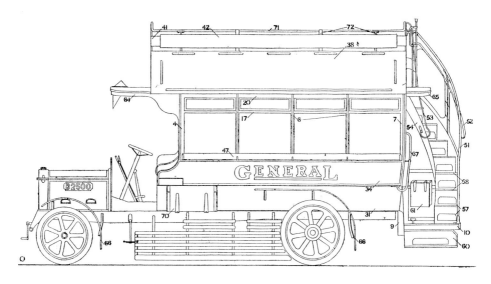

SIDE ELEVATION.

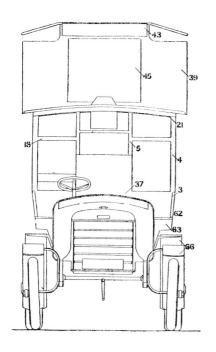

FRONT ELEVATION.

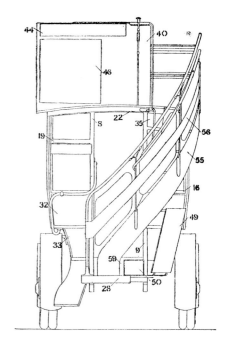

BACK ELEVATION.

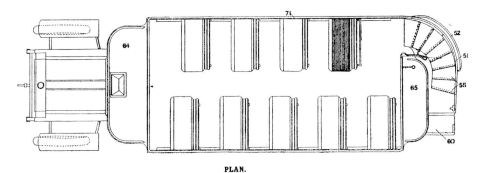

PLAN.

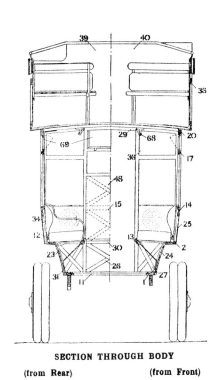

SECTION THROUGH BODY

(from Rear)　　　　　　　　(from Front)

FRAMING.

1.	Bottom side.	16.	Hind waist rail.
2.	Top „	17.	Side class „
3.	Front cab pillars.	18.	Front „ „
4.	Outer partition pillars.	19.	Hind „ „
5.	Centre partition pillars.	20.	Cant „
6.	Intermediate pillars.	21.	Front arch „
7.	Hind corner pillars.	22.	Hind „ „
8.	„ standing „	23	Side corker battens.
9.	Platform „	24.	Hind „ „
10.	„ bearers.	25.	Side panel „
11.	Floor „	26.	Front diagonal „
12.	Back seat rail.	27.	Hind quarter „
13.	Front „ „	28.	Platform „
14.	Side waist „	29.	Hoopsticks.
15.	Front „ „	30.	Front partition bar.

PANELS AND BOARDS.

31.	Side rocker panels.	41.	Top side fixture board.
32.	Hind quarter „	42.	„ „ destination „
33.	Rocker „	43	„ front „ „
34.	Side „	44.	„ hind „ „
35.	Top quarter „	45.	„ front route „
36.	Inside top quarter „	46.	„ hind „ „
37.	Front partition „	47.	Waist rail „ „
38.	Side advert. frames.	48.	Fare „
39.	Top front fixture board.	49.	Gate „
40.	„ hind „ „	50.	Police plate „

STAIRCASE AND SUNDRIES.

51.	Staircase hand rail.	62.	Diver's seat board.
52.	„ protection „	63.	„ heel „
53.	„ ascending „	64.	Front canopy.
54.	„ inside band.	65.	Rear „
55.	„ outside „	66.	Front and hind wings.
56.	„ tablet „	67.	Commode handle.
57.	„ riser.	68.	Tie rods.
58.	„ tread.	69.	Ventilators.
59.	Platform riser.	70.	Accumulator Box.
60.	Passenger step.	71.	Top guard rail.
61.	Ticket box.	72.	Roof standards.

"independents", their speed when lightly loaded and in skilled hands was remarkable. There was also a rear axle designated No.5 type with a ratio of 7.25 to 1 and 126 buses were at one period fitted with these. For the handful of conversions to chara-bancs there was a special axle with 6.25 to 1 ratio giving appreciably higher top speed.

On this chassis was mounted a double-deck body of a type already more or less standard in design and in use on the X-type and some earlier buses. It accommodated sixteen passengers face to face on upholstered seats in side and eighteen on forward-facing wooden slatted seats on the top deck, where each pair of seats had an individual canvas cover secured by straps for wet weather. There was a large driver's canopy, later fitted with a rain-deflecting leather-on-metal shield (no form of driver's windscreen was ever permitted) and a half-width roof at the rear for the conductor.

Small side-windows to the driver's seat, called for some reason "wings," were originally fitted, but as these made it almost impossible for the driver to give any hand signals the police refused to license buses fitted with them after June 1913 and they were thereafter removed. To provide support in their place for the overhanging roof, curved iron brackets were fitted to the bodywork just above the driver's head. The highest point of the body stood 12ft.5in. from the ground, the maximum width (at floor level of the upper deck) was 6ft.11in. which allowed for route-boards to be added on both sides of the body and the whole kept within the police regulation maximum of 7ft.2in.

The new bodies were built by the L.G.O.C. at their three coachworks - North Road, Olaf Street and Seagrave Road and orders for them also were given to outside builders Dodson, Hora and others, and use was made at times of serviceable bodies of older design taken off earlier type chassis as they were replaced.

These transfers were made at certain garages and details of this re-use of the bodies are given in the next chapter. The weight however was always an important factor and difficult to keep within the limits set by the police, and the B-type with the standard body weighed at first 3 tons 12 cwt, later reduced to 3 tons 10 cwt. In the nine construction years of the B-type bus many minor changes were made to the familiar body and experiments for greater comfort carried out.

It must he borne in mind that the latest contemporary London tramcar, the London County Council's E/1 class, was a large, fast, comfortable, totally enclosed vehicle and so there was every incentive to make the competing motor bus as attractive as possible in comparison.

Between 1911 and 1913 several seating layout experiments were made to try and permit the inside passengers to sit facing forward, but it was found that the minimum acceptable width for a double seat was 2ft.8in. and for a gangway 1ft.3in. (it must be borne in mind that this was an age of long and voluminous women's skirts) and whilst this total spread of 6ft.9in. was possible on the top deck with a slight overhang, it could not be managed on the lower deck between the rear wheels. In an effort to do this, a body known from, the method of its construction as "bentwood" was tried with lower waist panels and a rear wheelarch, but it was still found that only three passengers could sit comfortably facing forwards in it, on a single and a double seat abreast, and the idea was dropped, although a number of the trial buses built remained in service. They also weighed a full hundredweight

15

more than the standard bus, and their seating capacity was reduced to 32.

A modification of this idea, with flat but inclined side panels, was tried out in 1913 on B2578, and there was also an experimental wider body on B2649 after the War, and all-steel bodies had been tried in 1912-1913 on B1000 and B1425.

There were drawings for other designs including spiral-staircase and front-entrance ones, and factory photographs exist of trial structures, but it is not known if they were ever built, and certainly none entered service. Only on some large single-deck bodies built for B-type from 1920 onwards was a full-width body achieved with forward-facing seats, but by that time experience could be drawn from the new K-type which already had the configuration. Other minor bodywork experiments were a wrap-round driver's roof on B1384. and on a few others, and half-opening windows on B2029 (which may be seen on the large and beautifully made model presented by the A.E.C. to the Science Museum) but these were not adopted. Later bodies built in 1914 and again after the War had the main waist panel divided into three sections and used a lighter, open work support bracket above the driver's head.

In 1912 considerable thought was given to some form of side-protection at the wheels and several types of lifeguard were tried out. One design, on B455, involved carrying the front mudguards down to hub level joining them to the front of the rear mudguards by continuous iron sheeting at an angle but this was cumbersome, very heavy, and made servicing difficult. On the other hand a simple wirenetting cage to the rear wheels, tried on B129 proved too light to take shocks. In July 1913 a fence of six metal strips was fitted from wheel to wheel on B2058 and from this developed the final form of a side. lifeguard of a "ploughshare" type made of strong wooden slats designed to push an obstacle progressively outwards and clear of the rear wheels.

This type of side lifeguard was then fitted, to all B-type and to the surviving older types of bus still in use. Frontal protection for which contemporary tramcars had a well-developed and trouble-free system of a simple scoop that dropped on to the road on impact, proved in the end too difficult although many ingenious experiments were made from 1912 to 1915. Technical photographs exist of these, but the basic defect of almost all of them was their inability to compensate for the deflection of long leaf-springs under load or braking. B1016 had small revolving wheels in front of the front wheels, X40 had a wirenetting guard, B2029 had what are described as "Howard rubber rings", B2096 had a row of seven rubber buffers like very small wheels, B1027 had the same but with twelve, B2552 had a horizontal rubber tube and wire netting, and B2588 had a single rubber roller preceded by a brush on a stick in front of each front wheel. Research continued through the first years of the War, using the same buses; thus in 1916 B2026 appeared with vertical boards held on arms projecting from the axle-beam, but it would have proved impossible to keep rigid mounted as it was on an unsprung axle, and offered too small a ground clearance, besides posing the danger of interfering with the steering if struck and crumpled. X43 appeared with a similar structure, but with vertical rubber rollers.

These various versions were thoroughly tried out in service though, and the writer recalls seeing a Y-type Straker-Squire carrying a front guard reminiscent of an American locomotive "cowcatcher" on Route 52 in 1915.

B 1000 had an experimental all-steel body and was only used for Private Hire work.

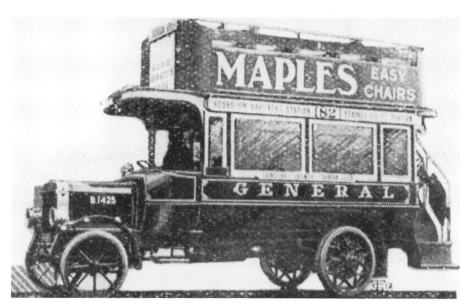

The second all-steel body was mounted on B1425 and intended for bus work but was not suitable for operation in Central London so it was relegated to the Hounslow and Staines route 82.

The London B-Type Motor Omnibus

One design which might well have succeeded came quite late,in 1916 when B3806 was equipped with what was almost an exact copy of the tramcar type - a front 'gate' with trip action and five horizontal wooden spars mounted firmly across the dumb-irons. This really would have worked, but at that stage of the War everybody seems to have lost interest in the matter and no further experiments appear to have been made.

Another type of protection to which a lot of thought was given was that from fire. The carburettor of the B-type engine was protected from overflowing by its simple float and needle device and there was an external tap to cut off the flow from the tank, but the few fires that occurred were expensive, though not particularly dangerous to passengers, who could alight from the other end of the bus. Full scale tests were therefore made in 1911 with a device known as the Grinell Sprinkler. In the first test A29, an old Milnes-Daimler, was set on fire at the engine, and most of one side of the body was destroyed, including one body-pillar burned completely through, before it could be extinguished. A second experiment on P35, an old Bussing, had similar results including burning the front tyre (the wheel however was of wood) but as a result of these tests a better type of extinguisher was developed, with jet action and a short flexible pipe for aiming. When this was tested by setting fire to X47, the fire was put out before either body or tyres were seriously damaged, and an extinguisher based on this pattern was used on all B-type thereafter save on the much later, post-war, large single-deckers which used the more compact 'Pyrene' type with pump action.

In the matter of lighting the 'General' lagged behind its competitors and up to 1913 used oil lamps or a cumbersome acetylene system. The gas generator was a large container on the driver's long bench seat for the calcium carbide and a smaller watertank above it. For many years no side or external lights were carried except for one large headlamp (sometimes two) beside the radiator on country services. It was evidently considered that even with the very modest interior oil-lamp lighting the buses would be amply visible by night.

After 1916 however police regulations required side-lamps and these (often still of the oil-burning type) were fitted on brackets to the dashboard. Electric lighting was gradually introduced from 1912 onwards, the current being generated by a dynamo with friction drive to the flywheel. A wooden box built under the body overhang at the front of the near side held the batteries. From the beginning lighting was also provided for the big destination-board set above the driver's canopy, at first by the acetylene system and later combined with the illuminated service-number box and stencils. Trial was also made with an illuminated side service-number on B1989 utilising one of the ventilator spaces above a side-window, (photographs show it was also found on B342 and 510) but this was not adopted, and indeed such a useful provision was not made for many more years, until the introduction of the S-type in 1920.

So far reference has been made only to double-deck buses as these made up the major part of the fleet. There were however routes on which by reason of a load restriction or overhead clearance single-deckers were needed, and five types of these were produced or adapted from 1912 onwards, seating from sixteen to eventually, twenty six passengers. These will be described in later chapters as they entered service. One of them, B1394, was used by the Private Hire Department and

18

was at first fitted with an older single-deck body with front and rear entrances originating from a 'Vanguard' Milnes-Daimler and later used on a De Dion. Later, B1394 was given the prototype "bentwood" single-deck body in 1913. Two chassis, B1354 and B1357, were fitted with open chara-banc bodies for private hire work, with full-length canvas roofs; as the name implies, these were truly "A-banc" for the seats were benches right across the vehicle with access only from the sides.

Other B-type built for special duties were the fleet of lorries and vans. The vans were wood-panelled and were used for carrying uniforms, stationery, tickets, posters and such items, while the lorries were open-bodied for stores and general duties. The open lorry-body of one, carrying the registration LN 299 seems to have been used for the road-testing of as yet unregistered bus chassis at Walthamstow. The early B-type lorries all had the coachbuilt wooden driver's cabs with an elegant curved side-piece, and only during the War and after did they receive plain cabs with stitched cloth roofing.

The London police were adamant in their refusal to allow any kind of top-deck covering though they had long permitted it to trams. It was not until 1923, when the NS-type designed by Owen Watson with a "cranked" steel frame and much lower centre of gravity was built, that they would ever consider the matter and even then two more years were to pass before the first covered-top buses were licensed, though they had been built for this from the beginning. However around that time one B-type double-docker was fitted with a covered top for tilting tests at Chiswick Works, and a K- and an S-type were similarly fitted, but as all three were painted grey and carried no numbers, their identity is not known. The writer saw them once only, on March 13, 1924, in the works.

Finally, the colours and livery of the B type should be described. Most of the fleet first ran in an overall dark red hue which had been adopted as standard since 1909. The same colour was also used by the 'Tilling' fleet of petrol-electric buses, which perpetuated it to the end. However following certain experiments in early 1913 the 'General' tried the lighter colour scheme of a brighter red, with off-white window frames and green lower panels, mainly on buses working from Hendon and Seven Kings Garages. Then after a few months the green panel was changed to one of chocolate brown. B1873 was one of the first noted in this final form, which became standard from 1914 onwards, and survived as the fleet livery for later types for many years.

Despite a uniform 'General' colour there was no lack of variety on the London streets since about one in ten of the B-type fleet carried at some period the colours of an associated concern. Alongside the red-and-white of 'General' might be seen the familiar B-type bus in blue and yellow for 'Central', in green and cream for the Metropolitan Steam Omnibus Company, in a light blue for 'Southern' and dark blue for 'M.E.T.', in various shades of green just after the War, and latterly there was a small but beautifully maintained fleet in dark blue and cream for the City & South London Railway.

This then was the B-type bus, slow, simple, open to the elements, but above all reliable and known and depended upon by millions of Londoners for work and play. Its reliability too enabled them to live farther afield from their work and also in a cleaner climate. Its profusion introduced the healthy social habit of taking a bus ride for sheer pleasure. The Londoner wrapped up well, climbed up into the wind on the top deck, ducked under the tarpaulin when it rained, surveyed. the woods and fields over the hedgerows, and came to know the beauty that surrounded him and made up London's country as never before.

CHAPTER 3

THE FIRST TWO THOUSAND BUSES IN SERVICE
G. J. Robbins

The growth of London's population in the first decade of the twentieth century had been considerable, but the lines of development were irregular, conditioned largely by the railways, whose courses in turn were set by topography. The population tended therefore to settle among the valleys radiating from the Metropolis, often with deep pockets of untouched higher country along side them. To a certain extent these wedges of higher land were served by the tramways, which had been electrified and could deal with fairly steep gradients, but a tramway route depended for survival, on a heavier population than did a bus route that could be varied at will, and many areas were thus left untouched until a reliable motor bus could open them up. The element of reliability needs to be stressed, for while, people would risk being delayed - or even stranded - on a weekend's pleasure outing to the country, the motor bus had to become accepted as thoroughly dependable before the public would entrust its everyday working life to it.

When therefore the new and more reliable motor bus had become available in increasing numbers, new routes were developed which linked railway stations and valleys of population as well as serving the country between them.

At the same time existing urban services were extended in some instances into country areas, principally at weekends but also where traffic showed promise for the full week. In 1911 the L.G.O.C. summer season guide showed thirty motor-operated services, (Routes 1-25, 27, 30, 33, 35, 36) most of them daily but with eleven additional services on Sundays to such places as Hampton Court and Epping Forest. Only two routes (32 and 34) were then still being operated by horse buses. In 1912 long country routes were introduced to places as far away as St.Albans, Windsor, Staines and Sidcup.

These new routes meant new habits. People who had seldom left London before save for an annual holiday by the sea now had an un-dreamed of service of access to their immediate countryside. In an age when urban air was far dirtier then the present generation can remember, the effect on a Londoner's health of such an accessible countryside can hardly be over-estimated. Nor was such travel any longer such an expensive proposition. The bus fares were normally cheaper than rail fares (though tram fares were often the cheapest of all) and the bus was, too, the first public vehicle that put the traveller off exactly where he wanted to be, and perhaps on this above all its popularity grew. In 1911 the L.G.O.C. issued an attractive bound guide book to London for Frenchmen, adorned with a picture of their new

B 9 was one of the new buses that started on route 25 between Victoria and Old Ford in October 1910 from the newly opened Clay Hall Garage.

bus and entitled "Londres vu de l'Imperiale an plein air partout".

It was the B-type bus that made such an impact on the London scene, and its introduction and development during 1911 and 1912 should now be considered.

Designs for the new bus had commenced in March 1910 although production of the 60 'X' type had barely started. On May 3, 1910 the L.G.O.C. Board authorised the building of 60 'Y' type buses. The decision to change the type letter from 'Y' to 'B' seems to have been taken subsequently as there is no other reference to 'Y' which was allocated in April 1911 to the Straker-Squires ex Great Eastern. B 1 at first was given the registration number LN 9970 following on from the 'X' type but this number was cancelled and when it entered trial service in London on October 18, 1910 the number had been changed to LN 4701. Eventually on October 31, B 1 together with eight other B-type ran on a new bus route from a newly opened garage at Clay Hall near Bow. The route numbered 25 ran between Victoria Station and Old Ford, and in accordance with the practice then in force the buses carried duty-numbers PA-A. PA-B, PA-C etc. onwards - 'P' the garage code, 'A' the route, and 'A', 'B', 'C' etc. the individual vehicles. Thirty three B-type were in service by the end of 1910, and the first sixty were all allocated to Clayhall Garage making up its full complement for the two routes, Route 25 and Route 8, the latter then working between Willesden and Seven Kings.

It would seem that even before the first went into service the Company was convinced that it had chosen the right type to build up its fleet, as during 1910 a batch of 167 registration numbers was obtained from the London County Council. These numbers were LN 4657-LN 4823, part of a series originally issued in 1907 but subsequently cancelled and thus re-issued three years later. They stopped short at LN 4823 as another company, the Metropolitan Steam Omnibus Company, had obtained LN 4824 onwards to coincide with its own fleet numbers.

This was in fact what the L.G.O.C. did as well all but two of the buses B1-B123 being allocated corresponding registration numbers LN 4701-4823. - the earlier registration numbers from LN 4657 following on afterwards. It is odd to note that this practice of obtaining registration numbers to agree with fleet numbers was not again adopted by the L.G.O.C. It was left to its successors London Transport to do this with trolleybuses some twenty five years later, and later still with 'Routemaster' and subsequent types.

The following list shows the date each order for building B-type was issued and the dates of delivery of the first two thousand buses. Each bus was valued at £345. The first two orders are for 60 each the same as the X-type.

Date of order	Quantity	Chassis No	Deliveries	
May 7 1910	60	B1 -60	Oct 1910 to Dec 1910	
Sept 29 1910	60	B61-120	Dec 1910 to Jan 1911	
Oct 10 1910	134	B121-254	Jan 1911 to Mar 1911	inc 4 lorries,
Jan 20 1911	253	B 255-507	May 1911 to Aug 1911	inc 3 lorries
May 15 1911	254	B 509-761	Aug 1911 to Nov 1911	inc 4 lorries
Oct 20 1911	254	B 762-1015	Nov 1911 to Feb 1912	inc 4 lorries
Jan 4 1912	3	B1016-1018	Feb 1912	light type lorries
Oct 20 1911	254	B1019-1272	Feb 1912 to May 1912	inc 4 lorries
Jan 29 1912	254	B1273-1526	May 1912 to Jun 1912	inc 4 lorries
Apr 27 1912	254	B 1527-1780	June 1912 to Aug 1912	inc 4 lorries
Apr 27 1912	254	B 1781-2034	Aug 1912 to Oct 1912	inc 4 lorries.

There seems to have been a break at B 254 as no new buses were delivered, in April 1911 thereafter larger orders are placed and delivery constant. Although 31 lorries are provided for in the preceding list it is known that 47 B-type were built as lorries or vans up to October 1912, fifteen of them being used at the Walthamstow works later known as A.E.C. The L.G.O.C. coach factories at North Road, Seagrave Road and Olaf Street were kept busy building bus bodies. Some were built by other companies, such as Christopher Dodson who supplied four a week at £130 each and Brush Electrical Engineering six a week at £140 each.

Following the registration batches used in 1910 the L.G.O.C. used even older numbers for B 174-212, namely LC 3813-3849, these being the balance of a series of fifty at first allocated to Arrow one of the Vanguard companies and not previously used. The General then obtained numbers LA 9801-9999 followed by five hundred in the series LE 9001-9500 for its rapidly growing fleet.

The second garage to to receive B-type was Cricklewood then coded 'E'. It was given 130 new buses to replace its older vehicles of a variety of makes but mainly Straker-Squires that ran on routes 1, 2, 16, also for new routes 13 and 18. After the completion of Cricklewood's allocation of buses which ceased at B 192 the next sixty two new buses were stored pending the completion of a new garage at

Turnham Green which was opened on May 8. 1911. No doubt time was also needed to train drivers and conductors. Thirty of the new buses were operated on the new joint working with Thomas Tilling Ltd on the revised 12 route between Turnham Green and Peckham put on to combat growing competition with National Steam Car Company. Ten days later a number of buses from this new garage were put on to route 7 which was extended from Wormwood Scrubbs to Shepherds Bush to serve the Coronation Exhibition at White City. On July 6. 1911 a number of B-type from Turnham Green garage went on to new route 27, Stoke Newington and Turnham Green. A new garage opened at Hackney in June also provided buses for the 27 and for another new route, 26 West Kilburn and Hackney Wick. On the last day of July Farm Lane and Middle Row garages each received twenty new buses for the new 28 route Wandsworth Bridge and West Hempstead replacing horse bus services.

Later in 1911 another new garage was opened at Holloway but by this time 'B' type - buses were replacing some of the older vehicles at other garages such as Battersea and Old Kent Road. The last 'General' horse bus was withdrawn from service in October 1911.

Two of the new chassis, B 75 and B 114 were taken out of sequence and allocated to the Company's Haulage Department, where they were given the lorry bodies and registration numbers LN 5994 and 5995 previously carried on Q type Thornycroft chassis. The registrations LN 4775 and LN 4814 being issued to later B-type. Soon afterwards three other lorry bodies together with their registrations LN 5996, 5997 and 5999 were transferred to new B-type B 175, B 201 and B 389.

Four buses stand ready to enter service on route 1 from Cricklewood Garage. B 142 has the body and registration number off a former Road car F-type Straker Squire, B 129 and B 131 have B-type bodies whilst the fourth bus is a Straker Squire still in use.

This transfer of bodies and registration numbers together applied also to some double-deck buses, the new chassis being sent to certain garages where the transfers were carried out.

The first of these transfers took place early in 1911 at Cricklewood Garage where B142 and B143 received bodies and registrations from former 'Road Car' Straker-Squires and B144 and B145 those from ex-'Vanguard' Milnes-Daimlers. These hybrid buses ran with other standard B-type buses on Route 1 and could be recognised by the smaller route-boards, above a single advertisement on the front, rather than the style adopted for X-and B-type vehicles.

This appears to have been a pilot scheme as in August 1911 six B-type chassis received bodies and West Ham registrations ("AN") from some former 'Great Eastern' Arrol Johnston buses then taken out of service. The six buses being B 426, 429, 430, 456, 457 and 464.

It appears to have been the intention that all the thirty bodies from the Arrol Johnstons, which had been taken off the road after only a few years of operation should be transferred to B-type chassis, a sufficient number of which (between B426 and B467) had been set aside for this purpose. The Arrol-Johnstons had Hora-built bodies of teak and though in good condition and not old may have been overweight, as after only six conversions the scheme came to a premature stop.

The remaining twenty four B-type chassis were fitted later with new bodies and then registered in the LE 90xx and LE 91xx series. The transfer of other older bodies to B-type continued throughout the autumn of 1911 and assuming the intention of including thirty from the Arrol-Johnstons, a total of a hundred transfers are noted, surely a premeditated figure. The balance of seventy were made up as follows:

From F-type Straker-Squire	32
From G-type Straker-Squire	8
From H-type Wolseley	8
From A-type Milnes-Daimler	14
From D-type Milnes Daimler	4
From E-type Milnes Daimler	4
	70

The seventy chassis for these transfers were taken from those numbered between B453 and B608, which were sent out to the garages where the transfers took place as required. The largest number were undertaken at Old Kent Road, which at that time was working a fleet of Straker-Squires. Here 21 of the bodies came from former 'Road Car' buses, they were B 458, 465, 469, 482, 488, 516, 535, 537, 554, 563, 567, 576, 580, 581, 593, 602, 603, 605, 609, 638, & 645. Nine came from former 'General' Straker-Squires B 461, 466, 468, 474, 497, 499, 502, 536, 546 and one -B 526 from an ex-Vanguard bus, One other chassis -B 508 also received a transferred body in 1912 the origin of this is not known. Eight conversions were carried out at Norwood Garage which had a fleet of G-type Straker-Squires being B 470, 489, 494, 495, 498, 611, 629, and 632. Some ninety Wolseleys operated from Battersea Garage and eight of the bodies were put on to the following new chassis, B 553, 584, 591, 596, 636, 637, 653 & 654.

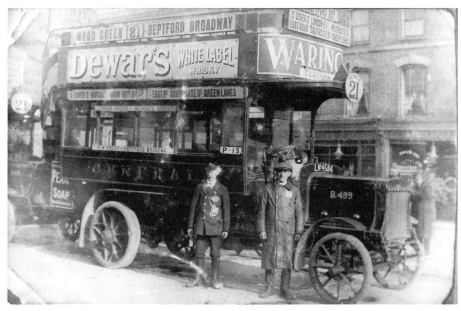

B 499 seen working on route 21 from Old Kent Road garage has the body and registration number from an F-type General Straker Squire hence the older style of route board.

Perhaps it is the Milnes Daimlers acquired from the Vanguard fleet that are the most interesting in this respect however. Fourteen B-type inherited very early A-91XX registrations first issued in 1905. They came from A-type Milnes Daimlers at Upton Park garage and were B 484, 485, 487, 610, 612, 617, 618, 627, 628, 646, 647, 656, 679, 686. The writer recalls seeing a B-type bus in 1925 with an A registration and wondered where this had come from as no such early numbers were then to be seen. Another eight with LC 50XX and LN 3XX numbers were transferred from former Vanguard buses of the D and E type, B 483, 486, 626, 648, 662, 666, 684 & 688. Although the chassis from which the bodies were taken were in many instances quite early ones, the bodies themselves may have been of later construction. They were later replaced by standard bodies during overhaul, but the registration numbers were retained thereafter.

In addition to B 508 ten other B-type B 728, 732, 733, 734, 735, 738, 743, 746, 749 & 754 were fitted with older bodies taken from withdrawn chassis and were allocated for training purposes being used for the instruction of new drivers from Monday to Saturday but available for normal passenger work on busy summer Sundays. About a year later in 1912 these eleven buses were joined by nine more mounted with older bodies these were B 1129, 1137, 1146, 1147, 1154, 1155, 1160, 1163, and 1164. All twenty were then given new registration numbers between LE 9887-9891 and LE 9901-9915. The original numbers of the earlier ten buses is not known. All were allocated to individual garages.

The construction of B-type chassis at Walthamstow gradually gathered impetus during 1911 and from the registrations allotted up to July appears to have been in order and at a steady flow of about forty per month, the increased number of chassis being supplied in the of latter part of 1911 covered partly by transfer of older bodies.

A large number of new bodies were however being built at the L.G.O.C's own coachworks, while many were supplied by outside builders such as C. Dodson and E. & H. Hora, but full details are not known. A change in procedure at this time was that registration numbers appear to have been given on the arrival of buses from the bodybuilders and not allotted in advance, hence the lack of any order after B425.

Even more spectacular progress was achieved during 1912, as in twelve months over fourteen hundred B-type chassis were supplied, double the number in the previous fourteen months. Eight new bus routes had been introduced during 1911, and by the end of that year route numbers had reached 36, with 51-57 in use for Sundays-only services.

The L.G.O.C. had completely absorbed the Great Eastern fleet by April 1911 when their routes were numbered 35, 36, and 37 the last was soon combined with L.G.O.C. route 8. They continued to be worked by Great Eastern vehicles but gradually these were withdrawn and replaced by new B-type commencing with thirty buses at Kilburn which ran on route 36. Lea Bridge Road and Russell Road supplied buses for routes 22 and 35 and early in 1912 the Great Eastern buses were replaced by B-type and in June 1912 these two garages were replaced by the new one at Leyton Green. The only Great Eastern buses to continue in service were the 'Y' type which ran on route 8 from Forest Gate garage. On June 20, 1912 the eastern terminals of routes 8 and 25 were exchanged, the 8 turning at Old Ford and the 25 (the original B-type service) running to Seven Kings. At the same time the A-type Milnes Daimlers at Upton Park garage were replaced by the 'Y' type from Forest Gate which then ran on the 25 route. Forest Gate was given a full compliment of B-type buses which ran on a number of local routes.

During 1912 nearly fifty new routes were started and by December the service numbers extended to 93, with 51-64 reserved for special Sunday operations. All the new routes were operated by B-type buses, although a few of the older types were still working. The growing fleet needed housing, and eight new garages were opened in 1912 and allocated B-type buses as and when required.

Changes in the style and fitments of the bus came in gradually. The first, which would not be apparent to the average passenger, was a change in the garage coding which up to November 1911 had been the three letter system developed from that used by the horse buses as explained earlier. For example, B14 is known to have operated with garage and duty code 'PA-N' - 'P' indicating Clayhall Garage, 'A' referring to Route 25 and 'N' being the duty on that route. On November 2 1911 all garage codes were revised and simplified, letters indicating the garage and numbers the duty, the route reference being omitted. Clayhall Garage became 'Y', so the example quoted for B14 meant this becoming 'Y-13' on Route 25.

A further change in the outward appearance of the B-type and other 'General' buses occurred in the summer of 1912 when the route numbers carried on large round white plates in black lettering, first used by 'Vanguard' in 1906, were replaced by route-number boxes, lit at night. and carrying numbers on metal stencils. All B-type buses were well supplied with route and destination indicators; the extreme destination was shown front and rear on the top deck, underneath which a larger board showed the names of the principal roads traversed, also front and

Two new country routes started on Sunday July 14, 1912. B214 leaves Harlington Corner for Staines on the first journey of route 45.

B 203 was completely full up with passengers when it ran the first journey on route 62 to Windsor Castle also on Sunday July 14. 1912

B 964 is standing at the West Hampstead terminus of route 28 in 1912. It is interesting to note how many route boards are carried on each side of the bus.

B 590, a Holloway garage bus is seen outside the 'Northcote' at Clapham Junction when working on the 19 in 1912.

rear, which districts rather than the streets covered were shown on long boards carried each side above the windows of the lower deck, with additional names on shorter boards on the windows and at the waist-rail. Also on each side of the top deck was another long board bearing in large letters the extreme destinations on either side of the route number. Curved boards were also carried across the front of the driver's dashboard drawing attention to special exhibitions or attractions on the route, while inside the bus there was yet another board listing stages and fares.

Thus at least thirteen boards and two route-number stencils had to be changed if a bus should be transferred to another route but fortunately buses in those days were as far as possible kept to one service.

An important change in London's bus operation took place in 1912, the L.G.O.C. being acquired by the Underground group, and the company was re-formed in order that the area of operations could be extended, permitting a radius of thirty miles from Charing Cross in place of the previously allowed fifteen. This led to the introduction of long country routes, mainly on Sundays and Bank Holidays, made possible also by the reliability of the new bus. Two new country routes commenced on Sunday July 14, 1912, when B214 from Turnham Green ran the first journey on new Route 45, Harlington Corner to Staines, and B203 from the same garage opened an even more spectacular new route, numbered 62, from Hounslow to Windsor Castle. Needless to say these new routes proved very popular. Similarly in the South of London Route 61 was inaugurated running from Brixton to Whyteleafe in Surrey.

The fact that the L.G.O.C. was now part of tho Underground group was emphasised too by the decision in the late summer of 1912 to introduce certain routes (numbered from 80 upwards) which started from outlying Underground stations and provided through connections from Central London by transfer from train to bus.

Routes 81 and 82 were in fact the Windsor and Staines routes renumbered, but others in the series were new routes, some only short but all on the outer fringe of London. The rapidly growing B-type fleet was thus being put to good use.

Sixty B-type were early in 1912 allocated to a new garage in Twickenham, opened in March, the first to have a double code-letter - 'AB'. It was allocated buses between B950 and B1290 and operated Routes 27 and 37. Soon afterwards in July another garage was opened at Chelverton Road, Putney, to which were sent some seventy new buses from those between B1647 and B1794. The same month a new garage on the other side of London at Palmers Green took a hundred new B-type bearing numbers between B1321 and B1660 to operate Routes 21, 29 and others.

During 1912 the L.G.O.C. used up the registrations LE 9750-9999 and obtained a thousand new numbers, LF 8001-9000, the largest known reservation of numbers for buses. which has not since been repeated in London. It showed the great confidence and the intended increase in the fleet.

Owing to the increasing number of bus chassis being assembled there the Walthamstow works, built in 1906 by Vanguard, had to be enlarged. In June 1912 the Underground Company decided that the manufacture of buses and parts should be separated from the operation of buses by the L.G.O.C. and that a separate company to be known as the Associated Equipment Company should be formed.

Thus the well-known firm of "A.E.C" was founded, and purchased the works from the L.G.O.C. but although the new company could now sell bus chassis to other operators, which the L.G.O.C. had not been able to do, it was to be another twelve months or so before any B-type chassis were available for outside sale.

For many years the L.G.O.C. had operated a small fleet of vans and lorries in connection with building and maintaining the growing fleet. All these additional vehicles were licensed separately from the buses by a special department that had its roots in the Haulage Department previously mentioned, and although it had ceased to supply lorries for hire it still ran a passenger private hire service and that department was responsible for charabancs. Separate small batches, taken out of those allocated to the L.G.O.C. were in use for vans and lorries, some examples being LE 9131-9149 and LE 9401-9420. Not all the lorries however were on B-type chassis, as those licensed in 1911 included several E-type Milnes-Daimlers; subsequently the bodies and registrations of these were transferred to new B-type chassis, three examples of this being B2036, B2037 and B2072. On the other hand some of the Straker-Squire and Milnes-Daimler lorries had in turn still retained their original registration numbers which later passed to the B-type. Thus B1021 bore the early registration number LN 336 and B1374 (which was an instructional chassis for some time) that of LN 299.

The B-type vans were allocated to various duties. Five of them passed to the Coach Factories -B453 to Seagrave Road, B717, B1027 and B1722 to North Road, and B723 to Olaf Street. Ten chassis B720, 726, 729, 731, 739, 753, 1016, 1382, 1729 and 1832 were retained by the works at Walthamstow and fitted with box-van bodies for lighter duties at the works, heavier work such as delivering castings being handled by Foden steam waggons. The vans passed to A.E.C. ownership after the separate company had been formed in 1912. During 1912 six B-type B 703, 724, 730, 1021, 1397, 1533 were known as ticket- vans being used for distributing bus tickets to the various garages. Another six B 1017, 1018, 1833, 2036, 2037 and 2072 were licensed for advertising and other publicity purposes. One chassis, B1247, had been retained for a time for instructional purposes but later in the year it was fitted with a lorry body and, along with B2060, was assigned to the London Electric Railway (part of the Underground group) and registered LF 9980-1.

In addition to the above each garage was given an open lorry for general duties though not all were B-type, the following are the B-type showing the code letter of the garages to which they were allocated The first five dating from 1911 most in 1912 others added 1913. B75 (Y), 114(W), 201(V), 389(H), 436(J), 437(P), 725(T), 727(F), 752(C), 1184(AB), 1374(G), 1387(G), 1391(AD), 1393(D), 1398(A), 1399(B), 1400(K), 1404(F), 1721(AF), 1728(AF) 1758(S) and 1831(AE).

Mention should also be made of certain B-type with specially adapted bodies for private hire work. First was B1000, a double-decker with almost "Pullman" style saloon body; B1354 and B1357 had 28-seat open charabanc bodies built by E.& H. Hora; B1394 had a singledeck enclosed body, taken from an N-type De Dion and previously on a Milnes Daimler of 'Vanguard' and last - to complete the five in this section - was B1499 vehicle was another double-deck bus for private hire work.

Prior to October 1912 all the B-type buses had borne the fleet-name 'General' but during that year other names began to be seen. By an agreement dated August 25, 1912, the L.G.O.C. undertook to run 55 motor buses for the Associated Omnibus Company which for some years had been operating horse buses in London, so the L.G.O.C. provided 55 B-type which were painted in the standard red livery but had

B 753 was one of ten B-type retained by the works at Walthamstow for general duties.

B 1021 was one of six ticket vans in use for distributing bus tickets daily to the various garages in the fleet.

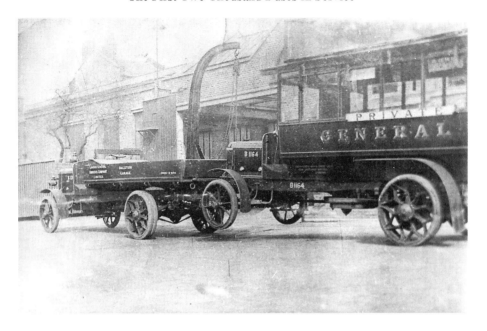

Each garage had an open lorry for general duties and B 1393, the Dalston garage lorry is seen towing a broken down bus to the garage. The bus is B 1164 one used mainly as a training vechicle.

the fleet name 'Associated' on the sides and the name of Philip Willing Tibbs as the Managing Director. These buses had registrations LF 9255-9309, and the first twenty two were allotted to Holloway Garage for Routes 29 and 43, then eleven apiece to three other garages - to Palmers Green for Route 29, to Albany Street for Route 24 and to Shepherds Bush for Route 11a. All were in service by the end of October and during the same month some more B-type appeared under another name, that of the Metropolitan Steam Omnibus Company which were operated by L.G.O.C.

Their fleet - some sixty Darracq-Serpollet steam buses - was replaced by B-type in the green, and cream livery of the company, with the fleet-name 'Metropolitan' on the sides above a coat-of-arms. Under an agreement of November 1912 the L.G.O.C. undertook to work one hundred buses for this company, all of which were allocated to the then recently opened garage at Willesden and operated on Routes 6, 8, 18, 46 and 66. They can be identified by their registrations LF 9310-9399 and LF 9421-9430. The Associated buses are listed in Appendix A against the letters 'AS' and the Metropolitan Steam buses as 'MS'.

Up to this time all London motor buses had been double-deckers, usually seating 34 passengers, but in October 1912 the 'General' wanted to replace the 'Tilling' horse bus route through Blackwall Tunnel by motor buses, but as these were higher than the horsed vehicles a single-deck type had to be provided to meet police requirements, so a vehicle which had virtually just the lower deck of the standard bus was produced. This had an open platform at the rear and held sixteen passengers, and reversible route-boards were fitted on to the roof back and front. The first nine

B 1394 was fitted with the saloon body originally on a Vanguard Milnes Daimler and used for Private Hire work.

B 1357 together with B 1354 had 28-seat open charabanc bodies built by E. & H. Hora in 1912.. B 1357 is seen in a country setting.

B 1917 was one of the 55 buses provided for the Associated Omnibus Company Ltd., and is outside Holloway garage ready for service on the 43 route..

B 2066 is one of a hundred B-type operated by the L.G.O.C. for the Metropolitan Steam Omnibus Company having the attractive green and cream livery of that Company. They ran on all routes from Willesden garage.

In October 1912 nine single deck buses having sixteen seat bodies were introduced for working through the Blackwall Tunnel on route 69. B 1879 is seen coming out of the Tunnel into Blackwall Lane.

of these buses were B 1817, 1828, 1871, 1879, 1881, 1918, 1919, 1925 and 1927 and all allocated to Athol Street Garage for a route between Poplar and Plumstead numbered 69 which commenced on November 21, 1912. After eight months it was found necessary to increase the frequency of the route, so another nine single deckers to the same style were built in April 1913. These were B 2215, 2218, 2219, 2221-24, 2242 and 2244.

A list of bus routes was first published by the L.G.O.C. in June 1910, entitled "Open Air to Everywhere" it listed motor bus routes 1 to 24 as well as horse bus routes 32 to 92. This was published monthly and from March 1911 it also included a map of motor bus services. Only a few horse bus routes remained. A regular feature was a calendar of events for the month and a list of bus routes serving such events. At the bottom of the map was the remark "The best way to see London is from the top of a bus" GLADSTONE. Each month during 1912 these bus guides had on the front a sketched picture of B 173 on route 18 and still carried the words "Open Air to Everywhere".

CHAPTER 4

CONSOLIDATION AND CO-OPERATION 1913-14
G. J. Robbins

Although a further six hundred B-type chassis were built during 1913 there was no longer the scope for spectacular progress that had obtained in the previous two years. A threat of competition had appeared in the form of the Daimler CC-type bus developed in 1912. The British Electric Traction group, which operated the Metropolitan Electric Tramways in London, had formed an associated company to work buses in conjunction with the tramways. This was called the 'Tramways (MET) Omnibus Company' and an initial order of 300 CC-type Daimlers had been placed. In November, however, the Underground Group and the B.E.T. Company formed a holding company entitled the London and Suburban Traction Company for the purpose of consolidating the interests of shareholders of Metropolitan Electric Tramways, London United Tramways and also the Tramways(MET) Omnibus Company. In May 1913 the South Metropolitan Electric Tramways and Lighting Company was added to the list.

In consequence when the first of the fleet of new "M.E.T." Daimlers appeared in January 1913 they were worked under agreement by the L.G.O.C. A small fleet of Daimler buses were already in operation in London as the British Automobile Traction Company (a B.E.T subsidiary) had ordered 33 CC-type Daimlers, the first of which went into service in October 1912. From January 1913 these olive-green 'British' buses which ran from a garage in Camden Town ran on routes 3 and 59. They were not worked by the L.G.O.C. although they came into the London Traffic Pool. From June 1914 they were moved to Route 24.

The original contract between the Daimler Company and M.E.T. agreed early in 1912 and covering the supply of Daimler bus chassis included also a maintenance contract for a period of three years for labour, material, petrol and lubrication. Bodies for the 300 Daimlers were to be built by the Brush Company to the design of Christopher Dodson. Two garages were planned to house this fleet, at Colindale and Tottenham, both within the Metropolitan Electric Tramways area. In October 1912 before any of the new buses had been delivered, it was decided that the 300 MET buses should be operated by the L.G.O.C. on behalf of the Tramways (MET) Company, the L.G.O.C..did not wish to continue with the maintenance agreement so this was given up in return for an increase in the total number of buses on order by fifty to a maximum of 350 chassis. In addition the Daimler Company was appointed selling agents for any surplus vehicles turned out at the L.G.O.C. Walthamstow factory where the B-type was built. Having increased the order for buses to 350 the MET reserved the requisite quantity of registration numbers namely LF 9450-LF 9799.

The first MET Daimler in a blue livery was licensed on 27 December 1912 and delivery of the other buses spread over the next ten months. In mid-January 1913 the MET accepted an offer by Daimler to substitute 100 B-type chassis for a corresponding number of Daimler chassis, the bodies for these B-type to be built by Brush but to the L.G.O.C. standard style. Three Daimler lorry chassis were also ordered but eventually one of these was changed to a B-type. The first MET Daimlers entered service on January 28, 1913 on route 1 from L.G.O.C. Cricklewood garage. MET buses were transferred to the new garage at Colindale when it opened in February 1913. Early in May 1913 the first B-type in MET blue livery was delivered and these were all allocated to the new Streatham garage and they became a familiar sight on routes 49 and 59 and others in South London. By the end of July Streatham had its full compliment of 99 buses and one lorry. Meanwhile further new Daimler buses were being delivered and the new Tottenham garage was opened on July 17, 1913. In June MET accepted a proposal from Daimler that a further 25 B-type be substituted for the remaining 25 Daimlers on order. The MET fleet was therefore completed by 25 standard B-type from the L.G.O.C. sales stock and they entered service between August 15 and September 9, 1913 allocated to Putney garage and ran on route 30. Thus the full MET fleet comprised 226 Daimlers and 124 B-type. Some Daimler buses were transferred to a new garage at Plumstead in October 1913. The L.G.O.C. did not wish to retain the Colindale garage as it was so near its own garage at Hendon, so it was closed in February 1914 its remaining Daimlers passing back to Cricklewood.

Yet another agreement was entered into by the L.G.O.C. in 1913 under which they agreed to work twenty two buses in London for the Gearless Motor Omnibus Company, and for this 22 Daimlers were placed in service from April 15, 1913. They were painted at first in a light grey livery with the by now rather inappropriate name 'Gearless' on the sides, but later many changed colour to the 'M.E.T' blue. These buses were at first operated from Hendon Garage on Route 13 and later they shared operation with the 'M.E.T.' Daimlers from Tottenham Garage. The Daimlers when delivered bore the large B.E.T-style number painted in shaded figures on the bonnet, but the L.G.O.C. subsequently added the type letter 'D' and used riveted metal numbers, D1-D228 being 'M.E.T' buses and lorries and D251-D272 'Gearless'

On August 29, 1913, ten B-type buses were placed in service in a light blue livery with the fleet-name 'Southern' and operated on behalf of the South Metropolitan Electric Tramways. These ten buses, B2271, 2275, 2285-2291 and 2294 with registrations LF 9946 to LF 9955, had been built some six months earlier but stored pending the agreement on their operation. The original order had been for ten Daimlers with Brush bodies intended for a route to supplement the company's trams from Mitcham to Belmont, and apparently the substitution by B-type was made by the L.G.O.C. These 'Southern' buses were first operated locally on route 59 but objections were soon raised by the Croydon Corporation on the grounds of competition with its own tramways. The 'Southern' buses were thereupon transferred out of the area, being sent to Twickenham Garage and later to Turnham Green, working on route 27.

D 172 one of the blue Daimler buses operated by the L.G.O.C. for the Tramways (M.E.T.) Omnibus Company Ltd., This bus working from Tottenham garage is seen at the Bermondsey terminus of route 4.

Another company taken over in 1913 was the London Central Omnibus Company, which ran a fleet of Leyland buses from garages at Walworth and Kingston, and also in Bedford. The twelve Leylands at Kingston which ran on route 71 (later renumbered 105) were in April 1913 replaced by twelve B-type buses in the 'Central' livery, they were B 2413, 2414, 2416-8, 2460, 2467, 2470, 2477, 2490, 2492 and 2514 and had registration numbers LF 9880 - 9891.

At the end of 1912 some ninety bus services were being operated, although the route numbers between 51 and 64 were allocated to special Sunday services, but in March 1913 the Sunday services were renumbered from 100 upwards so that the lower numbers were available for many new routes, introduced on a daily basis and operated by 'General', 'M.E.T' and other associated companies' buses. New garages opened in 1913 included Hendon (which was given new buses from B2201) and Seven Kings, Merton and Plumstead. 'M.E.T' Daimlers were sent, to Plumstead but the others had 'General' B-type, many of which had been in store until the new garages were available. The opening of new garages for the expanding fleet also caused additions to be made to the lorry and van fleet, and five new garage lorries were provided -B2296, B2530, B2570, B2614 and B2622 this last being attached to the 'M.E.T' fleet and allocated to Streatham Garage. Three new vans - B2480, B2555 and B2678 - were added to the Publicity Department fleet. At first B 2555 had been used for demonstration and experimental purposes at the Walthamstow works, and an official photograph shows it with registration number LH 8109. It never went into service in this form, the registration number was later issued to B 2675. In the meantime B 2555 was fitted with a box van body and given the number

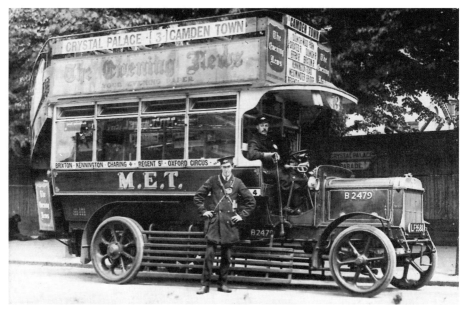

Replacing some of the Daimlers M.E.T. had 100 B-type in the summer of 1913 and all were allocated to Streatham garage. B 2479 is standing in Crystal Palace Parade when working on route 3.

LH 8128. Several of the vans and lorries mentioned had the bodies and registrations off earlier chassis, many from ex- 'Road Car' Straker-Squires.

Mention has been made of the agreement whereby Daimler were appointed selling agents for surplus B-type chassis. Between February and July 1913 the Daimler company were instrumental in selling 118 B-type chassis. These included 100 to Tramways (MET) Company in substitution for Daimler CC-type also the ten for 'Southern'. Their first sale to an outsider was of B 2329 in February but no other details are known. Two other unknown sales are B 2599 and B 2600 which had provisionally been registered as LH 8100 and LH 8102 so these numbers were later given to B 2661 and B 2668. Four B-type were sold by Daimler to United Automobile Services Ltd of Durham with double deck bodies. They were B 2623, 2628, 2639 and 2650 being given registrations AH 0138, AH 0139, AH 0140 and AH 0141. Having sold another twenty five B-type buses to tramways (MET) in July Daimler sold two more buses in August 1913 to the United Automobile Company B 2664 and B 2673 which were fitted with single deck bodies and registrations appear to have been AH 0187/9. All six of United's B-type were commandeered by the War Department in 1914, the bodies and registration numbers going on to other chassis after the war. One further chassis was sold by Daimler in October 1913 this was B 2751 which became a lorry for J. Carmichael of London, with registration LH 8716. The original number given to B 2751 of LH 8201 was used up later for B 3710.

The L.G.O.C. appear to have sold one chassis direct - B 2640. but no other details of it are known. One B-type chassis was sold at that time to the Metropolitan

Twelve B-type replaced some of the Leylands that L.G.O.C. operated for the London Central Omnibus Company in May 1913. The L.G.O.C. used them on certain routes during the busy Whitsun weekend before sending them to the Central garage at Kingston

B 2623 was the first of four double deckers sold to United Automobile Services Ltd., for use in Durham. It is seen at the Walthamstow works.

Asylums Board, fitted with a sixteen seat body off a 1907 bus registered LF 9923 and used as a staff bus. Whether this was B 2640 or one of the Daimler sales is not known.

B-type buses had continued to be licensed and put into service by the L.G.O.C. at a steady rate until B 2650 had been reached during June 1913, but this ceased temporarily during the summer months with B 2678, the last twenty being stored and put into service gradually during October and November of that year, although several had been sold as has already been recorded. It appears to have been a time when some experiments were taking place to improve B-type, particularly the bodywork. Early in 1912 an all metal body had been put on B 685 but nothing more is known of it. Although most London double-deck buses had the standard 34-seat body with the inside seats in the traditional longitudinal arrangement, attempts had been made to design a bus with the inside passengers facing forwards. This was achieved by a slightly wider body known as 'bentwood'(a technical term for the process of heating the wood in steam to form its shape) and the first bus built to this style was the private-hire saloon B1000, followed by B1425 which ran for many years on the Route 82 between Hounslow and Staines. Other experimental bodies were fitted to B1858 and B1873.

Early in 1913 another twenty 'bentwood' bodies were built, but it is not known on which chassis they were initially mounted except for five, B 2496, 2510, 2533, 2556 and 2514. These bodies seated 32 passengers, the forward-facing interior seats being double on the off side and single on the near. The buses were to be found on various routes, mainly from Putney and Seven Kings Garages, and their bodies were later stored during the War and afterwards mounted on twenty earlier chassis, B101(W), 185(N), 237(N), 301(AR), 561(-), 932(AK), 962(B), 1415(AR), 1418(AR), 1493(AE), 1518(Q), 1555(AE), 1614(C), 1662(M), 1700(AL), 1731(AL), 1873(B), 1897(CF), 2165(AK) and 2180 (B). The garages where known indicated by the code letters.

This 'bentwood' pattern was used in designing the prototype for a new twenty-seat single-deck bus, which in all probability was tried out in service late in 1913. It was a little wider than its double-deck counterpart, and two forward-facing seats, were fitted on either side of the gangway, twelve passengers sat in three rows facing forwards and eight more sideways over the rear wheels. There was an open platform at the rear, and reversible route-boards at front and back similar to those of the earlier single-deckers. The first body of this type was built early in 1913 and in September was mounted on B1394, which was transferred to the bus-fleet on the scrapping of its private-hire body which had dated from 'Vanguard' days.

This new twenty seat single deck bus appears to have been copied from a single deck Leyland bus designed by W. B. Richardson for the London Central Omnibus Company with similar seating. The first one of this style was put into service by the Central on the Kingston and Esher route in 1912 but a second bus was delivered to the L.G.O.C. Early in 1913 following the take over of the Central operations. B 1394 was allocated to Kingston garage joining the two Leylands on the Kingston - Esher route which was then numbered 79.

The supply of B-type chassis for London was resumed early in 1914 as the L.G.O.C. had placed an order for thirty single deckers to the bentwood pattern and 250 new double deckers, and numbers had been reserved for them between B 2679

B 1858 was fitted with an experimental bentwood body and a Leyland type dash.

B 1989 has an esperimental side number box and shows the new white and red colour scheme and the first use of the underlined GENERAL fleet name. August 1913.

and B 2959. Another single deck bentwood body which had some minor improvements over the prototype on B 1394 was built during the summer of 1913, at first it was mounted on B 2588 and had registration LH 8093. However this was the forerunner of the thirty new single decks on order and many were to be used on hilly routes so the standard B-type chassis was unsuitable and it was returned to the A.E.C. who provided the first of a heavier type of chassis with a more powerful engine. It was numbered B 2679 and it entered service in September 1913 no doubt on the Esher route. B 2588 was passed to Daimler and sold. The remainder of these buses were numbered B 2680 - 2708 and nine were delivered between February 26 and March 3, 1914 and were sent to Athol Street garage for route 69 that worked through the Blackwell Tunnel, replacing the older 16-seaters. Soon afterwards on March 29 this route was renumbered 108. The next four buses were stored at Plumstead garage from March 12 until a new garage at Catford was opened on May 11 when they were put on a new 112 route Penge and Bromley. Four were sent to Kingston garage to replace the Leyland single decks on route 79. Ten went to Holloway garage for a new route between Finsbury Park and Muswell Hill only suitable for single decks owing to steep gradients and a low railway bridge. After a spare was sent to Athol Street the last two went to Catford as one was needed owing to a contract to run a bus between Beckenham and the housing estate at Park Langley, this route was numbered 113.

In March 1914 the L.G.O.C. began to take delivery of the first of the 150 new double-deckers numbered from B2709 upwards, and up to August there was a steady flow of these, stopping with B2825 at the outbreak of the Great War, the first fifty going to Mortlake Garage to replace the De Dions. One modification about this time was the fitting of a "dished" front axle to give a greater clearance under the engine; B2749 is the first shown on official photographs to be fitted with this axle which thereafter became standard. The bodies still to the normal 34-seat pattern, were to some extent of an improved design and almost two hundredweight lighter giving an overall weight of 3 tons 10 cwt. The side panel was now divided into three sections, the window-frames were slightly curved, a lighter open bracket was fitted under the front overhang, and there were other small changes.

Only 112 buses with these new bodies actually entered service and little has been recorded of their use which was only for a few months - in some cases weeks - before withdrawal for war service.

It is believed that they had been intended as replacements for earlier. B-type buses which would then have become spares, as few new routes were commenced although several had been planned. Earlier in the year the 60 X-type buses had been withdrawn, the last in April, and no doubt but for the War the other non-standard types - Y-type Straker-Squire and L-type Leyland would have been replaced by B-type.

In March 1914 six new charabancs B3163-B3163 (though they did not carry their numbers) were added to the private-hire fleet on 14ft. wheelbase chassis and fitted with Daimler sleeve-valve engines. They were registered LH 8905-8910.

In March 1914 the special Sunday or country routes were again renumbered, this time in a special series from 151 upwards. Several outer suburban services were also renumbered; for example Route 54 was changed to 101, 62 to 103 and 69 to 108, thus releasing the lower numbers for new urban routes which however did not

The prototype twenty seat 'bentwood' body was mounted on the chassis of B 1394 replacing the old Vanguard Private Hire body. It is seen in Kingston Market Place working on route 79 to Esher.

materialise owing to the War. In October 1910 when the B-type had first appeared the L.G.0.C. had been running only 41 motor bus routes, which included two special Sunday services, whilst there were still some horse bus services, by August 1914 the highest London route number was 179, and there were 109 daily routes which included 24 outer suburban services and two all-night ones.

There were twenty one weekdays-only routes while on Sundays and Bank Holidays there were some twenty two special routes together with sixteen extensions of daily services. These special summer routes ran considerable distances, for example to Windsor, Dorking, Reigate and St. Albans.

To operate all these routes the L.G.O.C. and its associated companies had licensed some 3,100 buses, although 27 of these were temporarily withdrawn. Of this total 2,736 were B-type, in fleets made up as under:

London General Omnibus Company	2,435
Tramways(M.E.T)Omnibus Company	124
Metropolitan Steam Omnibus Company	100
Associated Omnibus Company	55
Central Omnibus Company	12
South Metropolitan Electric Tramways	10

To these must be added other bus types in the associated fleet namely 248 D-type Daimlers of the 'M.E.T.' and 'Gearless', 65 L-type Leylands from 'Central' and 51

B 2679 was the first of thirty single deckers with bentwood bodies, they all had only a few months service in London before being taken by the War Department for use as ambulances at the commencement of the 1914 war.

Y-type. Straker-Squires which had come from the Great Eastern Omnibus Company.

Certain bus routes were worked in conjunction with other companies, and Thomas Tilling ran 150 TTA-1 type petrol-electric buses, 'British' had 33 Daimlers identical with the D-type, and the National Steam Car Company had a fleet of nearly 180 green and white Clarkson steam buses.

London's licensed bus fleet in that fateful summer of 1914 stood thus at over 3,400 buses, yet daily operation was more in the region of 2,900, indicating the large number of additional vehicles retained in order that a regular and satisfactory service could be maintained. The L.G.O.C. had adopted the practice of laying off every bus at the end of ten days' working, which meant holding more reserve vehicles. Many more buses ran on summer Sundays and Bank Holidays, as the special country routes were to a large extent additional to daily operations.

CHAPTER 5

OUTSIDE SALES 1914
G. J. Robbins

Although Daimler had been appointed an agent for the sale of surplus B-type produced at Walthamstow by AEC not much progress had been made in this direction during 1913. Only eight had been sold apart from the 125 that had been supplied to Tramways (MET) company in place of CC-type Daimlers which were sold elsewhere and a similar action with the ten Southern buses. But the position changed in 1914 as the Walthamstow works had been kept busy building chassis for sale as lorries or buses for operators outside the London area, many being fitted with Daimler engines. These were largely Daimler sales and all the chassis were marketed under the Daimler name which appeared on the radiator whether they had Daimler or A.E.C. engines. For such sales it was deemed inadvisable to use the A.E.C. name in view of its close connection with a major bus operator. The A.E.C. name was used on a few sales made by L.G.O.C. By the beginning of 1914 some 200 chassis were made available to Daimler, the chassis numbers following on from the latest L.G.O.C. order which ended at B 2959. The chassis were in three sizes, B 2960-84 were 5-ton, B 2985-3009 were 4-ton and B 3010-3159 were 150 at the usual 3-ton range. Daimler had been fairly successful and orders for over 500 B-type had been obtained by the end of May 1914 although only 35 had been delivered at that time. The 3-ton range had been increased by another hundred numbered B 3169-3268 and later from B 3273 to B 3451. Some 4-ton chassis, no doubt against specific orders were B 3272 3453-62 and for 5-ton orders B 3463-72. The numbers were then carried on for 200 more 3-ton being B 3505-3704. Certain chassis appear at this time to have been supplied direct to the War Department. Of these it is reported that B 3012-3049 were open lorries, while about 275 were ambulances which duly went overseas during the war, of which only 45 returned to England, but it is not known what happened to them. By the end of October 1914 out of 700 B-type ordered through Daimler only 295 had been delivered, the outbreak of war in August 1914 causing cancelation of many outstanding orders.

The L.G.O.C. had 'earmarked' some B-type for their own use or for direct sales namely B 3160-68, B 3269-71, B 3474-3503 and B 3705-3803. A most interesting story arises from the sale of B 3160-2 as these three went to the Timaru Bus Company which operated in the town of Timaru in the district of Canterbury in South Island of New Zealand. It appears that the Borough Council had a single deck A.E.C. on trial and this led them to place an order in November 1913 for three bus chassis with Daimler B-type engines with poppet valves for delivery on board ship

B 2662 a standard B-type bus fitted with the new ploughshare lifeguard and the front registration number plate moved from the dash to the front of the radiator. July 1914.

within six weeks of receipt of order. This was for a 40hp double deck B-type bus complete plus two B-type chassis' built according to Scotland Yard regulations and fitted with continental tyres. B 3160 was the complete bus built by the L.G.O.C. as a standard- London bus and B 3161/2 the two chassis and these were despatched to New Zealand on January 13, 1914. Timaru Borough Council then built double deck bodies to mount on the two chassis as much as they could an exact copy of the General built bus. These three buses did very good service lasting until the early 1920s.

B 3163-8 were retained by the L.G.O.C. for the six charabancs as mentioned in the previous chapter. B 3269/70 were supplied in June 1914 to the Metropolitan Asylums Board and they were fitted with small second hand single deck bodies for staff use registered as LH 8992/3. B 3271 was sold with an L.G.O.C. double deck built body to A. Hutley of Coggeshall for a route between Braintree and Colchester. It was registered DU 5861.

Only limited information is known about the original sales by Daimler in 1914, as practically all were supplied under the War Subsidy Scheme and so many were requisitioned by the War Department. At least thirty B-type were ordered by B.E.T. for the various bus companies, in its group and many others were ordered later. An example is the eighteen B-type operated by the Northern General Transport Company. It had eight in May 1914 being B 3060 (J 2685), B 3061(J2681), B 3062(J2682), B 3069(J2686) B 3095(J2551), B 3096(J2684), B 3097(J2552), B 3098(J2683). Three more in June B 3099 (J2689), B 3127(J2688), B 3128(J2687). These were all 34-seat double deck but three others in August and September were

Three B-type buses were operated by Timaru Bus Company of Canterbury, South Island, New Zealand. One complete bus had been ordered as well as two chassis for which Timaru built double deck bodies.

30-seat saloons numbered B 3126(J3066), B 3216(J3068) and B 3222(J3067). The war intervened and though Northern had several buses requisitioned it was CC-type Daimlers that were taken and they kept the B-type. The last order was not completed until after the war when they were able to obtain buses returned by the W.D. so four were supplied between March and May 1919 namely, B 3092(J3072), B 3256(J3070) and B 3275(J3071). Some transfers took place between B.E.T. companies and four buses B 3185(HD195), B 3190(HD200), B 3191(HD201), and B 3203(HD197) new to Yorkshire Woollen District Traction Company passed to Gravesend & District Company in September 1914 to cover losses to the W.D. by the latter. Similarly B 3210 and B 3024 sold in July 1914 to Aldershot & District and registered as AA 5376/7 went later to Middleton Electric Traction Company, Mr W. P. Allen of Allen Motor Services that ran in Kent had two known buses in July 1914 B 3087/8 (LH 9002/4.) Daimler supplied another ten B-type to United Automobile Services in 1914 and it is believed the registrations were AH 0190-99. Four had saloon bodies and one AH 0199 had a double deck body off another bus. The others were charabancs and all but two went to the War Department. The survivors were one saloon AH 0194 and a charabane B 3025 which had the double deck body and number from another bus AH 0140. B 3110/11 went to Bournemouth Corporation registration numbers EL 2105/6 which were used later after these were requisitioned. B 3122 went to Mansfield & District Transport whilst B 3140 was sold to Rotherham Corporation in June 1914 as ET 796. Others were B 3063 to City of Glasgow (VS 219) and B3101-4 to Grimsby Tramways. B 3080-3086 are recorded as sold to an operator in Melborne, Australia.

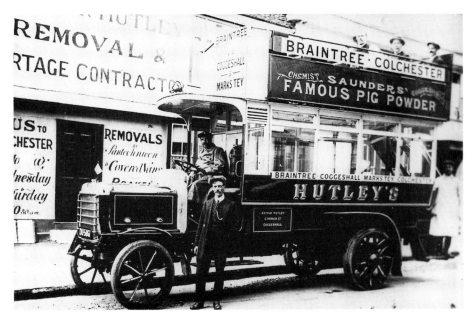

B 3271 was sold to G. Hutley of Coggeshall, Essex for a route between Braintree and Colchester, its registration was DU 5861.

B 3216 was one of a number of B-type sold to Northern General Transport Company, whilst most were double deck three including J 3068 had 30-seat saloon bodies.

CHAPTER 6

THE WAR YEARS: SERVICE OVERSEAS
J. B. Atkinson

The tension and excitement in London in the closing days of July 1914 contrasted oddly with busy enjoyment of summer sunshine and the lighthearted start of the August Bank Holiday weekend. The 'General' and its associates were working their buses at the summer peak of service, with special routes and extensions far into the countryside, and the great fleet of buses stood ready to take Londoners to the fields and woods, to the pleasant upper reaches of the Thames, to Hampstead Heath - in fact to enjoy "London's Country" at its best. At the same time there were crowds in sombre mood in Whitehall and Trafalgar Square anxious to know the worst if hoping to the last the threat of a war would pass. On Sunday, August 2, the Territorial Army was mobilised, and two days later threat became fact and war was declared.

It is doubtful if a placid and prosperous England had any idea of what was in store. Many believed, as well as hoped, that it would be all over by Christmas,and the mood of the time was one of intense patriotism but one well tempered with "business as usual" at the same time.

The first "casualty" to the 'General' bus fleet had occurred even before War started, as on August 1 the thirty single-deckers, seating twenty passengers and new only a few months before, were withdrawn from service for the emergency. Stripped of their interior fittings and hastily adapted as ambulances, they were on the way to Dover by nightfall.

In considering the part which the motorbus played in the War it must be remembered that, with memories of the Boer War only just over a decade before, the Army was still very much based on the horse. The elite were the cavalry. Supply problems were worked out in terms of the horse-drawn "Waggon, G. S." with its unsprung, steel-shod wooden wheels. The movement of troops was governed by their marching range carrying full pack, rifle, greatcoat and ammunition and supplemented, only in the rear by the railway with its covered trucks inscribed "Hommes 40. Chevaux (en long) 8" that were to be so un-comfortably familiar to the troops. The recruiting poster, even when carried on a motor bus. showed a man on a horse,

Fortunately however some at least of those who sat in the War Office had seen the need for mechanical transport and from 1912 small orders had been placed for motor lorries. In 1913 a War Subsidy Scheme had come into being whereby a considerable fleet of standardised vehicles of a few types - one of which was the

The D-type M.E.T. Daimlers were amongst the first of the London buses sent overseas in the war. D 70 is arriving in Ghent with wounded soldiers from Antwerp in October 1914.

B-type - could be mustered very quickly. Most of the 'General' buses built in 1913 and 1914 - that is, those from about B2360 onwards - came under the subsidy scheme and so were liable to be requisitioned.

When the war broke out it was however the Navy and not the Army who first asked for the loan of motor buses for the fighting area, and early in September a fleet of seventy D-type Daimlers was handed over to the Naval Brigade and, still in 'M.E.T' or 'Gearless' livery and manned by volunteer crews of the men who had been driving them shipped to Dunkirk. Once there the men were formed without further training into a unit of the Royal Marines and drove their buses in the initial advance to Antwerp, in the subsequent retreat from which most of the buses were lost, many being captured by the enemy. One contemporary account pays high tribute to these pioneers:

> The motor buses in Antwerp did a great work and all credit is due to the efficiency of the L.G.O. vehicles and their drivers. They absolutely kept the pot boiling the whole time by their incessant labour in feeding the troops with ammunition and food, not to say handling of wounded. The coolness of the drivers under a veritable hail of shell and shrapnel fire was an astonishing feature, and the fellows who had the good fortune to get through will have cause to be ever grateful for the manner our wonderful fleet assisted them.
> It was a sad sight to see the dear old M.E.T. buses battered about by the road side as we left them in our retirement.

This operation seems to have opened the eyes of the Army to the use that could be made of the ordinary motor bus as a troopcarrier, and fresh emergency in October 1914 put another three hundred buses into action at short notice. This time the men were mustered more prosaically into the Army Service Corps, two companies of which - the 90th. and 91st. - were formed and took 75 buses each to Avonmouth for shipment to Rouen, whence they moved forward to St.Omer to immediate action. This time the buses were all B-type, still painted red and carrying the familiar advertisements for Pears Soap, Maples furniture, and some of the current shows at London theatres one of which (it is said) was most appropriately entitled "One Damn Thing after Another".

These buses proved so useful, with their ability to move two dozen fully equipped fighting men into the line or from sector to sector in a time that disposed for ever of the old conceptions of mobility, that the Army now began a much larger troop-carrying operation based on them.

Requisitions of the buses had at first been regarded as loans to the Government but from October 11, 1914 all are shown as sales and the total given as sold on that date were 30 L.G.O.C. single deck, 94 double deck B-type, 219 M.E.T. Daimlers, and 22 Gearless Daimlers. Six M.E.T Daimlers which had been on loan to Manchester Corporation were returned on October 31 and then joined the other sales to W-D. Seventy of these Daimlers had been sent overseas as complete buses but the remainder were converted to lorries, the L.G.O.C. retaining the bus bodies which were put into store. In the last two weeks of October another 420 B-type had passed into the hands of the Armed Forces. Then between early November 1914 and the end of March 1915 a further 392 B-type were taken, 351 being from 'General' and 41 from its associated companies. In addition to buses the L.G.O.C. lost the chassis of eight charabancs but retained the bodies for further use.

The total of B-type chassis, including buses, lorries and charabancs, taken from the L.G.O.C. for war work was 954, about 550 of which were "subsidy vehicles". Of these last most were fitted with high sided lorry bodies, while at least ten became armoured cars. The lorry bodies were built at the L.G.O.C's three bodybuilding works and at some garages and the displaced bus-bodies were carefully stored in garages, mews and and other available spaces. The chassis or lorries went to a large W.D. storage depot at Grove Park Lee, along with the large numbers coming off the A.E.C' production line, and later sub-depots for this purpose were opened at Eltham and Catford, together with one for driver training in Osterley Park. Walthamstow built chassis carried the Daimler name but were otherwise standard B-type vehicles.

Although most of the buses taken over were sent overseas, several hundred were allocated to home services such as London defence duties, air-raid services, and hospital and convalescent home duties and these buses came from both the "subsidy" and the requisitioned fleets. One of these - B1441 - was noted at Brighton with convalescent Indian troops.

In France and Belgium the buses and lorries settled down to a variety of duties. As troop-carriers the buses could carry 24 fully equipped men. The windows were boarded up and the army numbers replaced (though not for some time) the original numbers, which were in some instances retained. Double-deckers served as ambulances for the lightly wounded, wireless equipment centres for the cavalry,

B 752 an L.G.O.C. lorry was rebuilt as an armoured car and used by the Royal Navy in 1914.

B 2132 was adapted as a travelling loft for carrier-pigeons.

Some London buses were retained by the war Department for various home dutes in England and B 1441 is seen here at Brighton with convalesent Indian troops.

covered transport for rations, and mobile lofts for carrier-pigeons (B2125 and B2132 are known to have been on this last duty). One driver wrote home in 1915;

> "We should often have gone short of rations had we not spotted the old B-type. They are holding their own with the best of them, bringing our supplies up from the depot. What struck me as comical though was to see the drivers wearing L.G.O.Co. badges in preference to those of their respective units"

As well as losing so many of the D-type Daimler fleet in the retreat from Antwerp, there were immediate casualties to both men and machines. One B-type bus that went from Willesden on October 14 was destroyed at St.Eloi on October 23 after carrying forward troops from the London Scottish Regiment to a disastrous charge. The driver wrote;

> "We were in a tight corner and had to get out quick and lively. The Major made several attempts to get the bus out but was unable to do so as it was between two fires and we had to abandon it after all"

The driver's excellent snapshot of this bus abandoned at St Eloi was later taken up by the A.E.C. and widely used for publicity with the legend "Born at Walthamstow. Died in France" See picture on page 56

The picture of the B-type bus abandoned at St. Eloi.

A month later another driver wrote.

"I have seen a few of our buses wounded here, in one the bonnet was at the back, It must have been hit by a 'Coalbox' poor thing. I don't think it will see London again"

Nor did these drivers' have only to drive. There were ambushes when they had to fight for their lives. One of the early contingents met trouble and the Evening News reported;

"At Armentieres some London bus drivers put up a brave fight when a convoy had been led into an ambuscade. The British were tricked here by German officers wearing British uniforms, but the Huns paid the penalty with their lives in the exciting 'scrap' that followed. One omnibus driver met a dozen marooned Germans eager to surrender when he was returning from a journey up the line with ammunition. He ordered them to get up on top and drove them back to camp"

As the war settled down into what was clearly going to be a long struggle along an almost static Western front, the importance of a mechanised transport service between railhead and trenches grew. As the Editor the L.G.O.C. staff magazine at the time commented:

"As a finished invention the London motor bus is a little older than the aeroplane and not as old as the submarine. As a war machine it is sharing the honours with these new devices. The British Army now in France is superior

56

in other respects, but it has undoubtedly a great advantage in possessing the finest transport men and machines, and it is becoming more and more recognised how much depends on the efficiency of this department"

Vastly increased numbers of troops meant - in Von Moltke's maxim that "no army food can be too expensive" - a gigantic problem of supply. For example the first Base Supply Depot at Boulogne which was feeding 66,000 men in 1914 had to feed 692,000 three years later, while another Depot at Rouen started with 17,000 and ended feeding some one and a quarter million men. While transport from Base Depots to Forward Supply Depots was by rail, from there on it depended on road movement.

Since every of the five British Armies needed two Forward Supply Depots, and as these were in the main set too far back to be able to rely on horsed transport to the Front, a very large fleet indeed of motor lorries had to be built up, and this in fact grew from the original 950 lorries of the British Expeditionary Force (many of which had come from the B-type fleet) to some 33,000, load-carrying motor vehicles by three years later, the majority of then used to serve the four big Forward Supply Depots at Wardrecque, Bethune, Doullens and Barlin. As part of this impressive fleet the B-type, shorn of the familiar bus body, were also used as field kitchens, armoured cars, field workshops, and even as mobile anti-aircraft gun carriages. These were fitted for the most part with old 13 pdr. guns from the Horse Artillery. which fired a 121/2 lb. shrapnel shell. A spring catch was fitted into the breech so that when being loaded at a high angle the cartridge did not fall out before the breech-block could be closed to fire. An extra strong return spring had to be fitted in to the recoil system to bring the gun up again after firing. The sides of the lorry folded to horizontal to provide a working platform while the chassis was jacked up for firing. Although the gun only weighed about 10cwt. it still imposed an enormous strain on the chassis, and a driver wrote home in April 1915:

"I got appointed to this anti aircraft gun section which consists of a quick -firing gun mounted on a B-type chassis, also Daimler ammunition lorries, a Star waggon, Wolseley car, and a Dingler bike. I have a kit of tools to fit with just about suitable to keep a few grass rollers and mangles in order with. One day last week we fired 126 rounds, you ought to see the old B-type buck-jumping when the gun fires, but she sticks it like a brick"

Three months of that however seems to have been enough, for in July the same driver writes:

"Our poor old B-type has at last given up the ghost under the strain of continual firing. Her chassis broke in the middle"

His accompanying photograph showed an unknown B-type with the large number 3668 on the bonnet side of the vehicle but this in not a B-type chassis number but a means of identification in use before an overall system of numbering W.D. vehicles was evolved.

For details of the antiaircraft guns the authors are indebted to 'The Guns of

1914-1918' by I. V. Hogg which gives a detailed account of their work. Mr Hogg points out that while perhaps only one enemy plane per thousand shells was brought down, the deterrent effect of the fire was far more important.

At first the B-type buses, which had been the first motor vehicles on the spot in any large numbers, were used for all purposes, and carried men, food, ammunition and petrol as needed, but with the growing number of lorries available it was possible gradually to reserve the surviving buses for troop-carrying and the movement of walking wounded. The original 90th. and 91st. A.S.C. Companies had been redesignated No.1 and No.2 Auxiliary Omnibus Coys. and had been joined by three more, and in October 1916 all five Companies were combined under G.H.Q. command as the Auxiliary Omnibus Park (MT), A.S.C. and were concentrated at St. Valery sur Somme for quick tactical use. The Auxiliary Omnibus Park had a War Establishment of 650 buses and other troop carriers, and the Companies could move at an hour's notice. It was claimed that a Brigade could be "embussed" in half an hour - and that it had once been done in four and a half minutes. The speed with which troops could be moved a given distance by bus was also carefully calculated as it was vital to know this. It was found that large bodies of men could be moved ten miles in the hour in convoy, or twelve by lone vehicles, in each case with a load of 25 men. Petrol consumption was assessed at six miles per gallon, and the range of action at 286 miles with 24 gallons of petrol carried spare in cans.

Movements of special note were those of the Twelfth Division into a gap at Albert in March 1313, and of a Guards Brigade into a breach near Strazelle, also the move by night of the Canadian and Australian Army Corps from Arras to Amiens for the final offensive in 1918. These were impressive feats but a tremendous strain on the drivers, who sometimes spent up to sixty hours at the wheel.

If the strain on the drivers was high, so was that on the buses, for most of whose maintenance the driver alone was responsible, yet many went through the whole four years of war with no other attention. One driver wrote with pride (and this was in 1919) that his vehicle had never been to Base, and indeed the B-type seem to have proved the toughest of all the lorry types used. While the repair manuals of the time list a long series of modifications needed for other makes, the only one suggested for the B-type (and that not a compulsory one) was that the engine compression could be lowered by placing steel plates of up to a quarter of an inch thickness under the cylinders.

This may sound crude indeed by present day standards but probably made for smoother running on the low quality petrol of the time. A significant minor point, noted not for modification but for attention on overhaul, was headed "Governers, defect in lubrication of" which suggests that these unpopular devices to limit the speed of the bus were not at all conscientiously kept in order by their drivers to curb speed.

Heavy repairs when required were originally done by an Ordnance Depot at Base, supplemented by a Army Service Corps Mobile Workshops Unit (usually itself on several B-type chassis) but later the A.S.C. took over its own repairs, setting up four repair shops. Two of these Heavy Repair Shops, located in Paris (St.Denis) and Rouen, cared for all Walthamstow products. Repairs undertaken include cylinder reboring, which was done with hand tools.

For the very large quantities of spare parts that were needed two Base H.T. Depots were set up at Calais and Rouen, No.1 Depot (Rouen) holding all supplies for the A.E.C. and Daimler vehicles. Towards the end of the War when every sort of material was in short supply a special workshop called a Retrieving Section was set up and recovered serviceable parts from wholly wrecked vehicles and forwarded scrap metal to St. Denis for casting of new parts. There was also a plant at Hesdin for pressing on new tyres. Compared with the figure of 33,530 lorries of all types in use, the total of 6,691 fully over-hauled by Base Workshops between 1914 and 1918 seems small, but it represented never-the-less a triumph of improvisation at times.

The sturdy nature of the B-type bus became legendary. It must be remembered that they had almost no asphalt roads to work on as a "good" road was the notorious Belgian 'pave' and the rest were the mud of the farm tracks of Flanders. Many of the Supply Route roads were only the width of a farmer's cart and as the supply system of the French armies used a plan of circular routes without regard to neighbouring British operations, columns of vehicles could meet head-on on a narrow causeway over a sea of mud and be heavily bogged down in trying to pass.

Maintenance was by any standards minimal and a bus could go through the entire war without overhaul. The drivers, who often remained with their original buses and developed an immense pride in them, would write home about this reliability, and the accounts written by two of then after more than four years' service are worth quoting. One driver wrote in February 1919:

> I left Grove Park on 22nd. October 1914 with the very same bus (B1219) as I had been on service with on the 67 route, Raynes Park to Liverpool Street. The beginning of November saw me and the old bus up at Ypres and from then onwards she has done good work by taking part in the first and the second battles of Ypres the battles of La Bassee, Neuve, Chapelle and Loos, did her bit in the Somme offensive and again at the battle of Arras, at Cambrai and also at Messines Ridge. Then again she did some good work in rushing reinforcements up to stop Jerry when he came in at Bailleul. One end of the line to the other was a long run but not too long for the old bus, which stayed the course and again helped to stop Jerry in his March offensive. And then we come to the final chapter and find her loaded with some of our brave Canadian troops chasing Jerry to Mons, and would have chased them to Berlin had not Jerry asked for peace when he did

Two veteran drivers, A. Redburn (who was later to found his own independent London bus company) and J. Davis, later wrote of their journeys with B58 carrying men of the Warwickshires, Cheshires and Middlesex Regiment into battle. They told of how they returned once from the battle of Loos festooned with German helmets. Of another bus, the driver wrote home in December 1918:

> I took over B2357 on October 23rd. 1914 at Grove Park, landed at Rouen the same month, proceeded up country on 18th. December after exchanging the bus body for that of a lorry box body and having from that date continued

B 490 and B 786 from Old Kent Road garage in use for the Private Hire Department helping to transport troops during the war years.

in charge of her till now. She has been riddled a bit with shell fire but still carries on and on the 17th of this month goes forward into Germany. She still has the good name of the reliable engine as when I first took her over and has never been to any base

Perhaps the last remark is the most revealing, showing as it does how these tough, slow-turning, engines defied wear. The story of this particular bus can be carried a great deal further too since after return to England B2357 served again as an "Emergency Bus" on the London streets for a year, and then after sale reappeared as a lorry in private ownership to give almost another ten years of service.

The various driver's letters quoted appeared in the "T.O.T. Magazine" the staff magazine of the Underground Group, and the considerable number of such contributions make this a valuable contemporary source for the attitude of what was still called the Rank-and-File of the time.

At the end of War the First Cavalry Division, which had some of the earliest of the buses in constant - if careful - use for the very vital purpose of forward wireless communication, had one completely stripped down for an engineer's report and this, listing every minor defect found, makes interesting reading. The results were good by any standard, and for a nine year old machine after four years of forward service and no workshop attention, remarkable.

Some frame rivets holding the cross members had stretched under torsion and worked loose, there was wear in the front axle swivel pin holes and in the front wheel bearing bushes, and some cracked spring-leaves and wheel spokes.

On the engine, two gudgeon-pins had worked slightly loose, the tappet-guides were worn and a main bearing cap-bolt had broken though remaining safely in place. On the clutch, elements of the forward ball joint had broken up. On the rear axle there was some wear in the bronze worm wheel. Details from 'The Automobile Engineer' of September 1920.

And that was all. Not one of the defects thus found had been sufficient to put the vehicle off the road for even a day in four years, so it is small wonder that their drivers trusted them and that often enough - as ex-servicemen after the War would put their gratuity into buying one on which to found a haulage business. Nor were the buses handled at all gently on the Flanders roads but were driven hard when the road - on rare occasions - was a good one. A contemporary account describes their speed when the road was good:

An officer related that one day he saw the bus transport on the move. Never before had he realised the speed capability of the vehicle. A train of them were en route for the front, each crowded with soldiers. The leader was a "go-er" and he was coming along at an exhilarating 35 miles an hour, the motor going for all it was worth. The man at the wheel was grinning and showing his undoubted delight at the chance to let the old girl out. But though he travelled fast he was too slow for some of those behind, the soldiers on the top deck of which were vociferously urging the leader to 'speed up his iron box

A few - both buses and lorries - went much farther afield in their war service. Double-deckers were noted in Athens and Thessalanike during the Turkish campaigns, and one driver sent a picture of his bus - B2411 - from Egypt with the unit's mascot goat on the bonnet.

The many letters that drivers wrote in their staff magazine at home reflect intense pride in their machines, along with a sense of personal involvement in tho war which is rather endearing; even the enemy was always a person, called Jerry, and the men would write (and the censor permit) some highly detailed and interesting accounts of their work and even of their moves, all laced with healthy humour and a nice disrespect for overzealous authority.

When it was all over and when demobilisation seemed agonisingly slow one driver sent home his plea in the shape of a photograph of his bus, which had been one of the first British vehicles to cross into Germany as it carried the wireless party of the 1st. Cavalry Division. The picture was of the bus still - in 1919 - carrying its original double-dock body, if much battered.

On the boarded-up windows were boldly painted details of the campaigns in which the bus had taken part. These read:

"1914 YPRES
1915 YPRES, NEUVE CHAPELLE, LOOS
1916 SOMME
1917 YPRES
1918 CAMBRAI
1919 COLOGNE"

- to the end of which its now war-weary crew had added the line:

"? LONDON ?"

Such was the service of the London bus in the time of need overseas. It is now time to look at the work of that part of the fleet that remained at home to carry the burden of serving Londoners in those war-strained years.

CHAPTER 7

THE WAR YEARS: ON THE HOME FRONT
G.J. Robbins

Turning now to what came to be known as the Home Front it is noted that, following the last call on the fleet by the War Department, the licensed fleet of motor buses had, been reduced by March 1915 to 1,886. Whilst the 'General' itself had supplied the greatest number of buses for war service, the 'M.E.T' had suffered proportionally the most severely, the War Deportment claiming 240 out of the fleet of 350 (226 D-'and 14 B-type) which left only 110 of the 'M.E.T' B-type for service. 'Associated' lost nine, the Metropolitan Steam Omnibus Company six, and 'Central' all their twelve B-type.

The loss of the thirty 20-seat single deckers to the War Department on August 1. 1914 was a sad blow to the operation of some routes. The L.G.O.C. still had nine 16-seat single decks numbered between B 2215 and 2244 and four of these were used for the Blackwell Tunnel route 108 which became Poplar and Greenwich only. Five more were sent to Holloway garage for the 111 route but as these were only 30 hp whilst those taken by the W.D. were 40 hp the route ran to the bottom only of the steep Muswell Hill. The prototype 20 - seater, B 1394 was left to keep up a very restricted service on route 79 to Esher. Due to the closure of Kingston garage, this bus was moved to Twickenham garage. Catford garage was also closed and routes 112 and 113 were withdrawn. There was an urgent need for more single deck buses so early in 1915 ten sixteen seaters were provided by converting some standard double decks to single deck. In addition to making more available for the 111 and 108 routes, seven were used to open a new route on April 26, 1915, this was 41 between Muswell Hill and Crouch End Broadway. The ten sixteen seat single decks were B 62, 79, 355, 358, 443, 947, 1229, 1317, 1836, 1842, and two more B 1574 and 1650 were added in July 1915 when 41 was extended to Wood Green.

Fortunately the L.G.O.C. had retained some earlier classes of bus that had been withdrawn from service in 1913 and 1914, including 46 of the X-type double-deckers which were now relicensed, as well as a number of the much older M-type De Dions, these being used for private, hire (in fact, mostly War Office work). In addition 20 L-type (ex Central Leylands) were brought back to London from the small garage at Bedford which was taken by the W.D. These Leylands joined 30 others at Hammersmith Garage where they ran on routes 11 and 74. At the outbreak of war L.G.O.C. had 60 B-type vans and lorries for various purposes, but nine of these had been taken by the W.D. namely B 75, 114, 389, 752, 1393,

1758, 2296, 2436, and 2481. At least one, B 752 became an armoured car. Nineteen B-type lorries were mounted with spare double deck bodies to increase the active bus fleet, they were B 201, 436, 453, 717, 723, 1027, 1184, 1247, 1374, 1387, 1398, 1399, 1400, 1722, 1831, 2036, 2060, 2072, & 2614. The lorry bodies were then mounted on older chassis such as De Dions. Eleven other former lorries, B 437, 725, 727, 1391, 1404, 1721, 1728, 1833, 2037, 2530 & 2570, were given sixteen seat single deck bodies and they must have been fitted with 40 hp engines as they were sent to Holloway garage for use on the 111 route which from July 2, 1915 was extended once more to the top of Muswell Hill. Further to augment the bus fleet, the nine A.E.C. vans B 720, 726, 729, 731, 739, 1016, 1382, 1729, 1832 were also converted to double deck buses and were additions to the M.E.T. fleet. Lastly, the one Y-type lorry also became a double deck bus. The one remaining private hire bus, the double-decker B1499, was fitted with a standard body and relicensed in April 1915, while B2622, previously a 'M.E.T' lorry, was given one of the spare 'M.E.T' bodies off the departed Daimlers. Two buses hitherto unlicensed (probably used for experimental purposes) were licensed, B2677 and B2826.

However by the winter of 1915-1916 the supply of new lorries for war purposes was for the moment considered to have caught up with the demand, and the L.G.O.C. were able to re-purchase from the War Department 108 buses which were rapidly put back into service, the 'M.E.T' receiving 39 of these and the other 69 going to the 'General' fleet. These returned buses included B1 and B2, and the subsequently preserved B340. Although most of the 108 were buses that had formed part of the L.G.O.C. fleet and so were given their former registrations, six had been lorries supplied by the L.G.O.C. to the War Department in 1916; four of these now resumed their earlier registration numbers which had been transferred with the bodies from older chassis - B3706, B3732, B3758 and B3769.

The other two B3744 and B3772 - were given new registrations, and B3710 was given the registration number from B2751 which had been sold by Daimler in 1913.

Heavier use, heavier loading, and shortage of spare parts focussed attention on the need to reduce wear and tear and experiments were made with devices to make the springing more progressive. It must be remembered that no form of shock-absorber for heavy vehicles then existed. Trials were made therefore with pneumatic suspension in the rear by large air cushions in opposed metal cups on B1060, and "bumping tests" were made over a period at Leyton Garage using B1290 after it had been bought back from war service, first in lorry form and then with the double-deck body. All this may also have been related to the over turning of B592 on the Epping road on September 27, 1915, as highly detailed photographic studies of the wheel track marks leading up to this were prepared. Tests were also made on ramps of up to three inches, approximating to kerb height, and it was found that rear wheels might be cracked in one or more spokes by a severe jolt of this kind.

The temporary lull in War Department needs also enabled the A.E.C. to supply some new chassis to the L.G.O.C., largely assembled out of stocks of spare parts held, and these were fitted with spare double-deck bodies out of store. The first six were numbered B3805, B3806 and B3813 - B3816, of which five went to 'General' and one - B3814 - to 'M.E.T' and therefore separately registered LP 8683. Then in the summer of 1916 twenty five new buses were supplied which bore the high fleet numbers of B6365 - B6889 and mostly carried 1914 - built "three-panel" bodies

The loss of the 20-seat bentwood buses to the War Department in August 1916 meant that some standard double decks had to be converted to sixteen seat single deck as replacements. One of them B 1317 is seen leaving the terminus at the bottom of Muswell Hill on route 111.

from store. Ten of them, B 6873, 6875, 6877, 6879, 6880, 6881, 6883, 6884, 6885, & 6887 were licensed as 'Gearless' on part replacement of the twenty Daimlers which had gone on war service. The B-type were painted in the standard red livery.

In May and June 1916 thirty new single-deckers B3474 - B3503 with 40hp engines were supplied, with 20 seat bodies identical with those of the earlier batch that had been conscripted as ambulances in August 1914. This order had been placed in 1914 but delivery delayed by the war, and by 1916 they were urgently needed to carry war workers engaged on munitions in Woolwich Dockyard and Crayford. They were wanted for four new routes - 99 between Poplar and Erith, 99a between Poplar and Crayford, 109 between Woolwich and Penge, and 110 between Dartford and Crayford. Although the first ten of the new buses were ready for service in May, the Erith police would not accept them for their area on account on their width, yet the Company was obliged to work Route 99 in the interest of the war workers as a subsidy was being paid for such a service.

The route therefore had to be worked for two months, by charabancs and such older single-deckers as the 'General' could muster. The L.G.O.C. had two Leyland charabancs and had retained, the bodies from the six charabancs - B 3163 - B 3168 - new in 1914 whose chassis had been commandeered by the W.D. Two of these bodies were now mounted on spare Leyland chassis and four on to four B-type chassis B 2830, 2832, 2834, and 2836 on loan from the A.E.C. Eventually the Erith police gave way and the new single-deck buses were able to take over Route 99 and following. the delivery of the remainder the other new routes were commenced. The

The Gearless fleet of Daimlers having been taken by the War Department ten B-type were provided in 1916 as replacements. B 6887 is seen after the war on route 48.

Although most of the thirty new 20-seat bentwood single decks new in 1916 were needed for the Woolwich routes two were sent to Holloway garage and so B 3480 is seen on route 111.

four B-type charabancs were withdrawn in August 1916 and their bodies were put back into store, but what happened to the chassis is not known; they may have been sold by A.E.C. and re-registered. During 1917 A.E.C. supplied L.G.O.C. with ten more B-type chassis from spare parts, these were numbered B 2850 - 59 and were fitted with lorry bodies.

The last additions to the wartime fleet were made in April and May 1917, the A.E.C. providing another ten B-type chassis from stock, B4869 - B4878, which had heavier frames and a longer wheelbases than normal - This was the result of some interesting developments before the War, at a time when the L.G.O.C. had wished to increase considerably the number of buses in use and the A.E.C. had been unable to meet this demand from its own resources. The A.E.C. therefore gave an order for five hundred motor bus chassis in parts from the United States, sending the drawings for manufacture to B-type pattern. Delivery was eventually made a few months after the War began when the War Department was taking about thirty buses a week from the Company but it was found that the American - made parts were appreciably heavier than their English counterparts. The Metropolitan Police would not license any heavier buses, being inclined to the view that the existing ones were already too heavy for the London streets.

In the circumstances the parts from America, which appear to have been allotted chassis numbers B4715 - B5214. were at first used as spares for existing buses. It is reported that some were sold to the Russian Government, and although the actual number cannot be confirmed it is possible that not more than forty could have gone overseas. The lorries for the Russian order, designated R- type in official records were two-tonners on shortened frames, with high, square dashboards and slanting louvres in the bonnet sides. A further number of these American-made frames and parts were used for War Office contracts for transport (perhaps from B4755 onwards) and for a few A.E.C. lorries (e.g.B4865 - B4868) designated Z-type. The ten chassis B4869 - B4878 were as previously mentioned used for single-deck buses needed to strengthen Woolwich Arsenal munition workers' services, being allocated to Athol Street Garage for Route 99 and to Streatham Garage for Route 109. Some older double-deck bodies were cut down to make 16-seater single-deck bodies for this purpose.

Spurred on by the need for petrol economy some study seems to have been made in July 1916 on reducing, rolling friction, and B6885 was tested with a calibrated towing-bar attached to the front to measure the tractive effort required to move the vehicle.

By the various expedients described, some, 272 serviceable buses had been added to the 'General' and associated companies' fleets during 1915 and 1916 but the shortage of vehicles was not the only worry at the time. Five of the Company's garages - at Plumstead, Camberwell, Catford, Tottenham and Shepherds Bush had been commandeered for war work. True, the fleet was much smaller and in consequence many bus routes had been withdrawn, mainly those of more recent origin. Some of the country routes were kept going as well as special Sunday workings which appear to have been considered necessary for morale in those days of hard work and extreme tension. There was also a shortage of crews as more and more men volunteered, or later were called up, for military service. Women conductors and cleaning staff were engaged for the duration of the war, and another wartime innovation was an increase in carrying capacity of the buses when the Metropolitan Police gave permission for standing passengers to be carried on the lower deck.

As an indication of the operation of L.G.O.C. buses during the war years the following list shows the running order of buses at Holloway garage on Tuesday, May 16, 1916. It will be seen that the odd numbers refer to early duties for crews and the even numbers the later ones as had been taking place prior to December 1911. Additional or extra buses operated when possible carry letters instead of numbers.

Route 4	Route 27	Route 42	Route 73
J1 B 1137	J1 B 1817	J1 B 529	J1 B 478
3 B 1124	3 B 1918	3 B 472	3 B 1176
5 B 1709	5 B 571	5 B 1152	5 B 1688
7 B 501	7 B 1666	7 B 1719	7 B 1316
9 B 1125	9 B 2614	2 B 1118	2 B 1102
11 B 922	11 B 343	4 B 1908	4 B 1677
2 B 524	13 B 530	6 B 948	6 B 499
4 B 568	15 B 510	8 B 493	8 B 1284
6 B 1117	17 B 991	*Route 43*	*Route 106*
8 B 1141	19 B 717	J1 B 491	J1 B 798
10 B 587	2 B 1818	3 B 475	3 B 474
12 B 326	4 B 1881	5 B 976	5 B 1652
Route 14	6 B 342	2 B 567	7 B 538
J1 B 2060	8 B 1879	4 B 799	2 B 1145
3 B 376	10 B 1191	6 B 754	4 B 1669
5 B 1140	12 B 371	*Route 43A*	6 B 1098
7 B 522	14 B 2224	J1 B1682	8 B 997
9 B 541	16 B 515	3 B1022	*Route 111*
2 B 1179	18 B 359	5 B 2346	J1 B 3481
4 B 368	20 B 525	7 B 723	3 B 727
6 B 512	*Route 30*	9 B 794	5 B 1728
8 B 532	J1 B 1910	11 B 883	7 B 2037
10 B 913	3 B 1921	13 B 1113	9 B 1391
Route 14A	5 B 1923	2 B 1115	2 B 3480
1 B 513	7 B 1928	4 B 1708	4 B 1721
3 B 1149	9 B 1166	6 B 357	6 B 1404
5 B 2018	11 B 1097	8 B 1951	8 B 2570
7 B 1161	2 B 1681	10 B 1952	10 B 437
9 B 1129	4 B 1920	12 B 1175	*Route 14 Extra*
2 B 1151	6 B 1926	14 B 946	JD B 1122
4 B 1174	8 B 1114	*Route 4 Extra*	E B 1950
6 B 514	10 B 349	J A B 526	*Route 42 Extra*
8 B 1172	12 B 462	B B 1712	JF B 1906
10 B 1138	*Route 27 Extra*	C B 570	G B 1148
	J A B569		
	B B572.		

Route 111 was allocated two of the new 20-seaters in addition to the 16-seat ex.lorries. Three of the double decks rebuilt from lorries feature in this list. Fifty eight buses shown above were allocated to Holloway garage when new.

During the dark days of war the A.E.C. factory at Walthamstow had been kept busy turning out chassis for the ever pressing needs of the War Department. In the opening months of the war and well into 1915 the chassis were all classified B-type though in different batches of numbers according to wheelbase and intended use. During November and December 1914 the L.G.O.C. had itself been engaged in completing an order for 200 lorries and vans for the War Department. These vehicles, which were numbered between B3705 and B3914, were assembled at certain garages taking either used or newly built bodies. B3705 - B3800 were noted as being War Department open lorries, and B3817 - B3874 as War Department box-vans, B3885 - B3902 as mobile anti-aircraft gun carriers. As well as these varieties of size and carrying capacity - two, three, and five ton models being produced side by side - there were other variations. Some were still produced with wooden chassis frames and some drew on the stocks of frames sent from the United States. Experiments were made with special types of wheel including, rather surprisingly, wooden artillery-type wheels on B3400.

During 1915 a sturdier design of chassis, with steel frame, curved dumb-irons, and sometimes fitted with 'Tylor' engines, had been produced, designated Y-type. These, as well as the B-type produced up to early 1916, carried the Daimler name on the radiator although built at Walthamstow, but the old agreement between the two companies expired that year and thereafter the direct sales including those to the War Department bore the radiator legend "A.E.Co."

The numbering of the Walthamstow-built Daimlers, though, referred to as the Y-type, was entirely within the overall pattern of chassis numbering which had started with the B- type and now intermingled the B- and Y-type in batches before the later runs of Y-, YA- and subsequent types.

B-type numbers appear to have continued up to at least B 3451 thereafter B 3474 - 3503, B 3705 - 3901, then B 4715 - 5134 which are those on the American frames. Another batch of B-type were B 6865 - 6889. Between numbers 3452 and 3473 also 3504 and 3591 were variations called 'S' or 'W' types. The chassis of the Y-type were 3592 - 3704, 3902 - 4714, then from 5215 - 6714, 6912 - 7369. They are YA type from 7370 also YB and YC from 7915 onwards. By 1919 the number 16145 had been reached. Some numbers were cancelled due to orders not being completed such as 5133 - 5214 and 6715 - 6864. For a time the post - L.G.O.C. B-type chassis continued to be given the big riveted numbers on the frame sides, even when carrying the Daimler name on the radiator, but when wartime mass production got going in ernest, this identification was reduced to a small stamped brass plate fixed to the off side frame member.

The A.E.C. later claimed that by the end of the War more than ten thousand Y-type lorries had been supplied to the three armed forces. Proof of their value to the war effort was the fact that they represented more than 40% of the entire supply of lorries to the Forces. The Y-type was a robust vehicle powered by a 45 h.p. engine, had a pressed-steel frame in place of the B-type's wooden one, and a heavier. four-speed, "crash" gearbox designed specifically for heavy load carrying. The production of so many of these chassis was a major feat, the enlarged

In April 1917 the A.E.C. provided another ten sixteen seat single decks and B4870 is seen carrying munition workers on the 109 service between Penge and Woolwich.

Walthamstow factory having developed a moving-track assembly line unique in the country.

The Associated Equipment Company was justifiably proud of this highly efficient method of production, and the contemporary press enthused warmly over the technique which produced a lorry every half hour of the day. An idea of the growth of the factory is given by the increase of the original floor area of 3,000 sq.ft. in 1906 to 483,000 sq.ft. by the end of the War.

With the A.E.C. fully engaged with this vast production for the War Department, it is somewhat surprising that they were able to supply even a few chassis to the L.G.O.C. as already noted, yet by June 1916 the Company had been able to increase its fleet, so badly depleted when the War started, by about 355 vehicles. In the end however all this was of no avail, as submarine warfare had seriously reduced the supply of petrol which was controlled and placed on ration from August 1916. Thus the average number of buses that could be worked was considerably reduced as a further number of vehicles were taken out of service. First the Y-type Straker-Squires were withdrawn from service in August 1917, then the X-type were placed in store during November and lastly the L-type Leylands were withdrawn on December 2, 1917. The L and X type were later relicensed but the Y-type did not return to passenger service many becoming lorries. Also during April and May 1917 fifty B-type buses were withdrawn to be converted into lorries for the Government. One bus, believed to have been B948, was withdrawn and used in the training school as instructional chassis.

The driver and woman conductor of B 1131 are seen wearing their summer uniforms. The bus is standing at the Richmond terminus of route 33.

Women were also engaged in cleaning the buses and they are busy making a good job of cleaning B 1260 in Willesden garage.

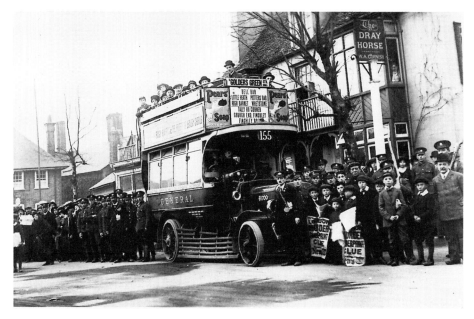

Although most of the special Sunday routes were withdrawn when war started a few did continue into the summers of 1915 and 1916. One of these was the 155, Golders Green and Hatfield. B 1700 a bentwood bus is seen one Sunday at the 'Dray Horse' Hatfield.

Experiments for substitutes for petrol were made but without very much success. Coal gas would operate the engine provided it was fed in at an even pressure, but storage on the vehicle was the difficulty. In July 1918 some B-type buses were fitted experimentally with a balloon-silk coal-gas container occupying the whole of the top deck. They appeared to run well when the "balloon" was full but then as the bag emptied it would thrash wildly from side to side like a sail and become dangerous. Several were nevertheless seen in service along the Hammersmith Road, but since it in any event reduced the seating, capacity by half an had a range of only about twenty five miles the device was given up and trials made instead with gas in cylinders.

For this purpose B533 was fitted with four (later changed to two) cylinders of compressed gas at 1,100 lbs. per square inch, stored under the seats of unsuspecting inside passengers. A main reducing valve, incorporating the cut-out device, reduced the pressure to 2lbs. per square inch and fed a flexible expansion chamber from which it was piped to the carburetor. A small auxiliary petrol tank was retained for starting. The expansion chambers were located behind the front destination board and were only about six inches thick so the whole fitting was very compact. During August 1918 twenty buses were fitted with this equipment and gave satisfactory service for the few remaining months of the War.

London was subjected to air-raids from 1915 onwards, twelve by Zeppelin and nineteen by the more dangerous aeroplane, and on September 8, 1915 two buses were badly damaged by enemy action. They were B804 from Willesden on Route

London was subject to air-raids in September 1915 and B 2273 was damaged and sent back to Hendon garage for repairs.

8 in which the crew and some of the passengers lost their lives, and B979 from Mortlake Garage. Both buses were fitted with replacement bodies from store and returned to service later in the same month.

The 'General' fleet thus continued at this low ebb until to the relief of all the Armistice was signed on November 11, 1918. This led to a day and night of wild excitement in London, scenes never to be forgotten, as jubilant crowds swarmed on to the bonnets and cab-roofs of long suffering buses and cast down paper streamers and even the wooden roof destination boards to feed bonfires in the streets.

Four of the many women conductors employed during the first World War are standing alongside B 1134 the Chelverton Road garage training bus.

B 1436 one of a number of buses comandeered by the War Department and fitted with a lorry body for war service overseas.

CHAPTER 8

POST WAR. ADDITIONS AND EXPEDIENTS
G. J. Robbins

Problems and difficulties were experienced for some time after the end of the War and the L.G.O.C. made immediate efforts to augment its bus fleet. Already by 1919 certain of the withdrawn routes had been reinstated and new ones introduced. The first additions to the bus fleet were 32 B-type lorries which were fitted with spare double-deck bodies out of store and relicensed for passenger service. Most of them had been converted to lorries in 1917. Then in 1919 the Company were able to obtain some new B-type buses, incorporating some of the spare parts manufactured in the United States as described in the previous chapter. By the end of the War only sufficient sets of parts (and these only to the extent of 60% in completeness) remained to allow the building of 250 buses.

The consent of the Metropolitan Police to the modifications involved for the new - and somewhat heavier - vehicles was not granted until after lengthy negotiations had been completed in November 1918 and a prototype bus - B4879 - had been constructed by the Company at Willesden Garage for this purpose. The Company also assembled three lorries - B4880-B4882 - at the same garage for the London Electric Railway.

The work of constructing and completing the new buses was then put in hand by the A.E.C. which built 250 chassis - numbered B4883-B5132 - between December 1918 and April 1919. The majority of these were fitted with bodies of the three-panel design which had been in store or partially built when the war broke out and were later completed, but in addition several new bodies were built by the L.G.O.C. to the same style to complete the batch.

These new buses, which were designated 'Type 7', entered service between February and July 1919, all being allocated to the Cricklewood, Hendon and Willesden garages and worked on Routes 1, 2, 6, 8, 13, 16, 18, 28, 84 and 142. They had a more powerful engine and were distinguished in appearance by the polished aluminium dashboards, which led to their being nicknamed the "Silver Queens".

In another attempt to build up: their fleet the L.G.O.C. approached the War Office to repurchase B-type buses or chassis which were still in reasonably good condition. At first only just over a hundred were found suitable but eventually 165 were bought, these being vehicles which had been in use by the War Department on home service. By June 1919 sixty-two of these had been fitted with bus bodies and were. able to re-enter service in London.

However still more were needed and at the end of May 1919 the Metropolitan

One of the 250 New B-type buses. New early in 1919. Note the aluminum dashboard which led to them being nicknamed "Silver Queens" B 4909 had been involved in some kind of experiment.

Police consented to relax the strict conditions of licensing for a limited period and permit as a temporary measure substandard vehicles. This led the L.G.O.C. to obtain another 230 buses or chassis from the War Department from those returned from overseas and from May 31, 1919 to place into service a number of "Traffic Emergency Buses". Some two hundred of these were painted green or rather a colour known as khaki, with the fleet -name 'General' in white on the sides and the words "Traffic Emergency Bus" were painted in small letters on the near side panel above the back wheel. Many still had the bodies that had been used on war service abroad and had only had a brief overhaul replacing such items as the window glass and upholstery.

In addition there were nearly another hundred red "Traffic Emergency Buses", these being sub-standard chassis but with the. standard red-painted bodies taken from those in store including some from the former 'M.E.T' Daimlers. The first twenty had bodies taken from the Y-type Straker-Squires recognisable by the curved white canopy over the 'driver' s cab.

The bus B43 later, to become famous as 'Ole Bill'. and be preserved as an example of the buses that had served the country so well in the War, was one of these "Red Emergency Buses".

Not all the emergency fleet however was from the War Department as fourteen were converted from the Company's lorries. these were some that had become lorries in 1917. Another eight, B 2850-2, 2855/7/8, 4866 and 4868 came from lorries that were new in 1917. These were noticeable for their larger non-standard type of

B 537 in the khaki paint of many of the Traffic Emergency buses.

Only four of the thirty 20-seat bentwood single deckers returned to London service after the war. One of them, B2705 is seen at Penge in 1919.

dashboard. Seven khaki and seventeen red emergency buses were converted from surplus 16-seat single deck buses. The category in which the repurchased buses went into service, i.e. khaki or red is shown were known in Appendix A.

The majority of the "Khaki Emergency Buses" came into service between June 1919 and January 1920, the red ones being added at a slower pace between November 1919 and May 1920 and during 1920 several khaki buses changed colour to red. The number of emergency buses in service gradually declined from the summer of 1920 onwards, until the last fifty were withdrawn early in January 1921.

One reason why the L.G.O.C. needed the extra buses in 1919 was the withdrawal in November of that year of the National Steam Car Company fleet of Clarkson steam buses, the 'General' allocating B-type to the four routes they had worked. None of the steam buses were acquired but seventy of their bodies were purchased, painted Khaki, and mounted on ex-War Department chassis. One known to have carried such a body was B42.

Included in the "Red Emergency Buses" were four single-deckers B2687, B2693, B2701, and B2705 which were the only remnant of the thirty twenty-seaters taken by W. D. in August 1914 to return to London service.

The L.G.O.C. had thus been able to repurchase from the Government some 504 chassis, more than half of the total it had lost in 1914-1915. Of these, 108 had been obtained in 1915-1916 and the rest in 1919. Understandably, many of this last batch were in poor condition and 38 of them were considered unsuitable for passenger work and were fitted with lorry bodies, replacing B-type lorries that then became buses, and also other types such, as the M-type De Dion and the Y-type Straker-Squire, which in turn were sold. The Y-type had been in store since 1917 and did not re-enter service; twenty one of them had become lorries, whereby their bodies became available for transfer to the B-type chassis as already described.

The thirty eight lorries from the War Department were given fleet or reference numbers running from "41/152" to "41/189". It seems that these numbers had been introduced in the war years, possibly in connection with petrol rationing. Some of the L.G.O.C. ticket-vans were similarly numbered, the batch "41/10" to "41/12" being carried by B703, B1018 and B1017. Eight other vans had continued in their normal duties through out the War but their "41/" numbers are not known. They were B724, 730, 753, 1021, 1397, 1533, 2480, and 2555.

Another expedient to increase London's immediate most-war bus fleet was the relicensing of the remaining L- and X-type buses, both of which types had another year or so of useful life. Lastly, mention must be made of the "lorry-buses" which were A.E.C. Y-type lorry chassis with Tylor engines, carrying lorry bodies adapted to seat 27 passengers on wooden plank seats, the whole body being shielded in bad weather with a tarpaulin canopy. A total of 180 of these were on loan from the Government and were licensed in June and July 1919., and then withdrawn in the middle of January 1920. They were registered by the Company in the then current batch of numbers between LU 8036 and LU 8216, and painted grey over all. All were returned to the A.E.C. and the registrations cancelled in 1920 except for eight, which were retained and given new charabanc bodies for private-hire work, and twenty which were fitted with double-deck. or single-deck bodies and sent to 'East Surrey'. The remaining chassis were re-sold by the A.E.C. to other operators.

With the end of the war the Government had withdrawn the subsidies paid for

The B-type buses of the Tramways M.E.T. Omnibus Company changed its fleet name from M.E.T. to METROPOLITAN by 1920 as shown by B 822.

the munition work services, with the result that Routes 99, 99A and 109 were withdrawn early in 1919 and a number of single-deck buses then became surplus to requirements. Many of the twenty-seaters, new in 1916, were then transferred to Holloway Garage to work Routes 41 and 111, and the old sixteen seaters withdrawn from service.

Twenty four of the latter were converted to red or khaki "emergency" double-deckers in late 1919 or early 1920. Fourteen of the sixteen-seaters were however relicensed during 1919-20 for further service due to the revival of Route 109 in September 1919 and of Route 99 in July 1920. Also in the autumn of 1919 there were another sixteen of the twenty-seat 'bentwood' type available for use; four were the ones returned the War Department as already mentioned, and twelve were new bodies built in 1919. Six of these were mounted on chassis of former double deck khaki emergency buses namely 2850-2, 2855, 2857 and 2858 and two which had previously been lorries B 2854/9 and four on those of former sixteen seaters B 1229, 1574, 1721 and 4870.

The maximum post-war total of B-type buses, single and double-deck in London was reached in June 1920 with a figure of 2,627 which included 126 red and 196 khaki "emergency buses". The fleet still retained buses of some of the associated companies - 46 'Associated' , 10 'Gearless' and 10 'Southern' but the 94 surviving buses of the Metropolitan Steam Omnibus Company had been absorbed into the 'General' fleet and that company had been wound up. This enabled the Tramways (MET) Omnibus Company to change its fleet-name from the unattractive initials 'M.E.T. to the name 'Metropolitan'.Its dark blue livery had by 1918 given place to the standard red,and the total fleet in June 1920 was 175 buses but in August 1920 a further 63 B-type were transferred to 'Metropolitan'to increase the total to 238.

Almost as soon as the War was over the Company had begun to implement its plans for an improved design of bus for the post-war fleet, the result being the 46-seater K-type with wider body and forward-facing interior seats. K1 went into service on August 4,1919 and K2 a month later. Following the success cf these two, another thousand were built during 1920 and 1921 and these quickly took over the main Central London routes from the B-type, whose numbers in service now began to decline.

The National Steam Car Company Ltd., having sold its London operations to the L.G.O.C. in November 1919 transferred its activities to Essex and developed routes based on Chelmsford and Bedford . The latter was made possible as the L.G.O.C. handed to National the garage at Bedford which it had acquired from the London Central Omnibus Company in 1913 and which had been in the hands of the War Department during the war years 1914-19. National withdrew all its steam buses replacing them by A.E.C. YC-type which were numbered in a new series from 2001. Therefore the name of the company was changed in February 1920 to National Omnibus and Transport Company Ltd.

The L.G.O.C. having experienced difficulty in operating certain country bus routes from a garage at Watford found a solution in National acting as agents for operating such country services. Therefore an agreement was signed; whereby National should operate a number of routes north of London on behalf of General who supplied the necessary vehicles. 'this commenced on May 13, 1921 when the L.G.O.C. handed over to National the garage at Leavesden Road, Watford, with its fleet of fifteen B-type buses. These were all of the 1919 -built Type 7 being B 4896, 4902, 4914, 4917, 4920, 4924, 4930, 4931, 4937, 4938, 4960, 4972, 4992, 5037, and 5072. They were working on routes 143, 145 and 147 later renumbered N1 to N3. A week later another ten B-type buses were loaned to National in order that other routes around Hatfield, St Albans and elsewhere could be developed. These were older buses but three more type 7 passed to National in July 1921 B 4964, 5025 and 5027. Although owned by the L.G.O.C. these were, at first painted in the 'National' white livery inherited from the Steam Car days, but later a red livery was adopted for these buses on loan, and all were returned to the L.G.O.C. between 1922 and 1928 although a few had been replaced in between these dates.

The L.G.O.C. made a similar agreement with the East Surrey Traction Company of Reigate for the operation of buses south of London, in Surrey and Kent, the L.G.O.C. supplying the garages and vehicles and the 'East Surrey' operating them under its own fleet name. The first three B-type were transferred to East Surrey in May 1921 and went into service on a route between Farnborough and Sevenoaks. Nine more B-type followed in August when the route was extended to Bromley North Station and numbered S2. Another route S2B commenced at the same time between Farnborough and Sidcup. A garage was built for them at Dunton Green in 1922. The 'East Surrey' found these B-type, buses not powerful enough. for the hilly roads of its area as the buses were all of the older 30 h.p. variety and. so the L.G.O.C. replaced them with others of the 40 h.p. type, which, though pre-war vehicles had had their earlier engines replaced by the more powerful type. The first were sent to Reigate in September 1921 and gradually during the next nine months

A number of 'Type 7' buses were operated by National Omnibus and Transport Company north of London on behalf of L.G.O.C. from 1921. B 5025 with a body off a National Steam Car bus was seen at Bishop's Stortford on 29 July 1922.

B-type buses were transferred to 'East Surrey' as required by the development of new routes.

By May 1922 'East Surrey' were operating 29 B-type, all on loan. The first fifteen or so had all been in the blue livery of 'East Surrey' but from April 1922 the standard red colour was adopted which facilitated the transfer of vehicles. The hilly terrain of the North Downs however still proved rather beyond the strength of even the 40 h.p. B-type so the L.G.O.C. sent to 'East Surrey' twenty A.E.C. YC-type chassis fitted with Tylor engines that were some of the former London "lorry-buses". Fourteen of them were given spare B-type double-deck bodies and the other six new single-deck ones, and these were used on the extra hilly roads of Routes S3, S6, S9 and S10 (later renumbered 403, 406, 409, and 410). The 'East Surrey' was also operating a number of Daimler and A.E.C. YC-type buses of their own in addition to those on loan from the 'General'. A similar number of K-type buses were supplied to 'East Surrey' in 1923 and most of the B-type then returned to the L.G.O.C.

Twelve B-type however were retained into 1924, and one additional one borrowed from April to June of that year. Only six were retained into 1925.Three were bought by 'East Surrey' for disposal. Meanwhile the heavier Tylor-engined buses from the A.E.C. remained in service until 1927,

Bonnet numbers of buses loaned to 'National' and "East Surrey" are given in Appendix A.

The London B-Type Motor Omnibus

Late in 1920 the L.G.O.C. built the prototype of a new and improved single-deck body for the B-type chassis seating 26 passengers and based on the successful K-type bodies then being built in large numbers.

The new body replaced a double-deck one on B4900 and entered service before the end of the year on Route 99 between Woolwich and Erith. The forward-facing seats were similar to those in the K-type, and headlights were suspended from the driver's canopy as on the K-type double-deckers. Another 74 of these 26 seat bodies were built in 1921 and all mounted on 'Type 7' B-type chassis whose double-deck bodies then joined the "body float" and later were to be seen on other B-type of the fleet.

Sixty two of these new single-deck buses commenced operation on six routes between February and May 1921, replacing 47 twentyseaters and 14 sixteen-seater buses then in use. These six routes were Routes 41, 79, 99, 108, 109 and 111, but unfortunately the new buses proved unsuitable for the Muswell Hill Routes 41 and 111 owing to weight restrictions on railway bridges in Crouch Hill and Crouch End Hill (one on each route) where for many years no buses with more than twenty seats were permitted. Therefore in June 1921 the new buses were withdrawn from these two routes and replaced by a similar number of twenty-seat 'bentwood' pattern buses put back into service. Some 22 of the twenty-six-seaters were in July available for new routes or for route extensions in the Kingston area and other parts of London, four were handed over to 'National' for working routes from Watford Garage and eight were reconverted to double-deckers. Two months later another

The East Surrey Traction Company Ltd., operated a number of bus routes on behalf of the L.G.O.C. who supplied the buses. This commenced in May 1921 and B 1214 and B 2126 are seen in Dunton Green garage for the S 2 route, Bromley and Sevenoaks.

The prototype of a new and improved single deck body was built in 1920, and had seats for 26 passengers facing forward. It replaced the double deck body on B 4900. This bus entered service on route 99 Woolwich and Erith not the 41.

three new single-deckers passed to 'National' and ten more were built for new 'General' routes.

A far-reaching development in the L.G.O.C. operation took place in 1921 with the opening of Chiswick Works. This will be described in the next chapter, but since it eventually absorbed the driver training school a word should, be added about this. Up to 1914 drivers had been trained by garages locally most having buses allocated solely for this purpose, but in that year a Training School was set up at Milman Street, Chelsea. This provided a driving area, part of which could be used for skid-control practice, and there were wooden reproductions of traffic-islands, and a movable contrivance of scaffolding of the full height of a bus to simulate overhanging buildings or lamp-posts and teach drivers to allow for the tilt of the bus on cambered roads.

The practice appears to have been for garages to send their own buses allocated for training bringing their own trainees, and the respective buses, along with some stationed permanently at Milman Street, provided sufficient vehicles to simulate traffic conditions on the training ground. A photoqraph taken in August 1919 shows that Milman Street School had the double-deckers B192 and B1353 of its own, while Norwood and Holloway Garages were using single-deckers B4872 and B62 respectively. Skid-control played an important part, with the smooth solid tyres of the times and the even smoother London roads of tarred wooden blocks liberally laced with slippery tramlines.

In addition to vehicles for driving,an instructional chassis was usually kept in an indoor classroom. At Milman Street this was successively B1247 (until this

B 5099 was one of the new 26-seater single decks passed to National to operate from Watford garage on routes such as N 16 Watford and Harrow Station.

became a lorry) B2567 (either loaned by or bought from the A.E.C for whom it had been a pre-war demonstration chassis) and probably B948 from about 1917.

The end of 1921 saw London's bus fleet back to its prewar elegance, the lorry-bus and emergency bus gone, replaced by increasing numbers of the new K- and S-type vehicles. The B-type however still made up more than half of the total fleet. Much of its flamboyant display of route-boards had disappeared. The long boards that originally covered the small fanlight windows had gone as long ago as 1913, replaced by a longer one each side below the windows. The practice of indicating the terminals on long boards either side of the top deck was given up early in 1921 and then in common with the K-type the older buses carried only the route-number on the sides of the top deck.

CHAPTER 9

THE WORK OF THE BUSES 1922-1925
G. J. Robbins

That the B-type buses, most of them by now ten or more years old, could give up to five years more of hard public service was due in a large part to the new concept of overhaul introduced when the L.G.O.C. opened its Chiswick Works in 1921. Hitherto an annual overhaul had been carried out in the garages, which was wasteful in holding spare parts, wasteful in time (the average period was sixteen days) and wasteful in holding skilled personnel locally for small numbers of vehicles. Such an overhaul comprised a general check of the whole bus, replacement of worn parts, decarbonising the engine and repainting by hand.

At Chiswick however a far more drastic overhaul took only four days (ten years later the time had been reduced to two) and here indeed the Company profited to the full from its early policy of standardisation, On the arrival of the bus at Chiswick its body was lifted off by a hoist and the chassis driven from under it on to a moving, line, called a ropeway, where it was systematically stripped of its major components and assemblies. The radiator, engine and gearbox were removed in turn, then the front and back axles on their wheels, then the springs, and the remaining bare frame was carefully examined for faults and for condition of the timber between the flitch-plates.

Satisfactory frames were stacked for re-use and the assembly process started on another ropeway, receiving overhauled units from other conveyor-lines at right angles, the assemblies coming from their own repair shops as ready and without regard to origin. This had the result that differing but interchangeable parts might reappear on the oldest or the newest chassis - pointed or flat-topped radiators, seven - or eight-spoked pairs of front wheels, straight or dished front axles for example - and of course any of the several varieties of body that stood next on the line for use.

The whole operation was very carefully timed, the different ropeways running at speeds of from four to fifteen inches a minute, and was sufficiently flexible to permit simultaneous assembly of all four types of chassis which after 1923 were in use. Indeed the system was so flexible that on one occasion the entire programme was suspended for a week and a fleet of Dorman-engined small vans known as V-type and of the Company's own design, built in the works, to replace the ageing fleet of Ford Model-T vans.

On overhaul, since all the units were repainted in their own shops before going on to the ropeway, the chassis was ready when it had received its last component; for the B-type this was the set of bonnet-covers with blank number-plate, on to which loose digits of the number were now riveted. The chassis would by then be standing over a pair of powered rollers in the ground, by which the engine was started through the back wheels. The chassis was then driven off for a short test and for adjustment of brakes, and then to the body-shop for the next available body to be mounted.

The overhaul of the body, which was also very thorough, took a good deal longer. A typical item was the removal of all the floor slats, whether worn or not, and their replacement with new wood for passenger safety. The painting of large surfaces was speeded up by what was known as the flow method, a forerunner of modern spray-painting technique, in which paint was literally poured over the lower deck from containers with perforated nozzles very like the domestic watering-can, and the spillage collected from troughs on the floor and re-used. This was not as wasteful as it might sound since it was found that one such "flow-coat" was equal to two applied by brush. Hand painting was still used for the upper deck, and the finished body was given several coats of clear varnish for protection and smartness.

As by now there was always an excess of bodies over chassis available, there was no delay, and a bus would be back at its garage inside a week from leaving it. This had a noticeable effect on the general appearance of the B-type bus which hitherto had undergone little change on overhaul but now seldom left Chiswick with the same body as it had previously carried.

One result was that during the last five years of operation the 1919-built buses could be seen with early styles of body, and vice-versa the three-panel bodies on much older chassis. Undoubtedly this interchangeability of units assisted in prolonging the useful life of the type.

In 1922 eighteen more twenty-six-seater single-deck bodies were built and mounted on older chassis which were then fitted with the more powerful engine which enabled them to be used for the same work as the previous 'Type 7' buses, that is those in the B 49xx- B 5xx batch. These older buses were B 62,122, 489, 622, 632, 790, 925, 1289, 1614, 1722, 1743, 2027, 2036, 2175, 2227, 2243, 2807 amd 4866. Several new single-deck routes were introduced on the fringes of London, and another five buses went to 'National' on loan, bringing their single-deck fleet up to twelve. In May 1922 a lighter variation was produced when one of the twenty-six seat bodies was cut down and given an open platform, in place of the closed back of the larger type, the seating capacity being reduced to twenty. This body was fitted to B1058 which then joined the other smaller buses on Routes 41 and 111.

In November 1922 the chassis-frames of B 1574, 3475, 3476, 3480, 3493 and 3499 being six of the 'bentwood' single-deckers were lengthened so that they could be fitted with the cut-down twenty-six-seat bodies to carry twenty passengers. By the end of the year another twenty two of the twenty-six - seater bodies had been adapted to twenty-seaters to replace the 'bentwood' bodies. Increases however in the frequency of the two Muswell Hill routes late in 1923 meant that more twenty-seaters were required.

There was now a surplus of the larger twenty-six-seater - type, so twelve of these were cut down in order to conform with the reduced weight and seating capacity. During 1923 another eight new twenty-seat bodies were built, these having a slightly curved lower panel instead of straight sides as previously. Two of these bodies were mounted on the chassis of former doubledeckers - B442 and B1659 - these being the last B-type to be converted to single-deck. Finally, another six completed the conversion of the 'bentwood' type. The total of twenty-seat buses thus reached 55, operated on Route 41 from Tottenham Garage and on Routes 41, 110 and 111 out of Holloway. All these, as well as the larger type, were running on hilly routes and so were fitted with a sprag-gear preventing running back, which had to be engaged before climbing any steep gradient.

Six of the twenty-six-seat buses operated on Route 71 between Lewisham and Croydon and for a few months they were operated by Thomas Tilling from their Croydon Garage. This ceased in November 1922 when Route 71 was withdrawn, but Tillings came back into the B-type picture in May 1924 when eleven twenty-six-seaters for Route 109 between Penge and Chislehurst were worked by Tillings from their Bromley Garage as there was no 'General' garage convenient to this route. The buses remained in 'General' livery though they had Tilling crews and carried the code 'TB' of Bromley Garage on the sides. These B-type were replaced in October 1925 by new Tilling-Stevens petrol-electric single-deckers, at first in the 'General' livery.

In the summer of 1922 the City and South London Railway, the earliest of London's "tube" lines, needed modernisation involving the enlarging of the tunnels and called on the help of motor buses to maintain their traffic during rebuilding. The work began with closing of the Euston-Moorgate section on August 9, 1922. Sixteen B-type buses were loaned to the railway, painted dark blue and lined out in white, and bearing on the sides the legend 'Auxiliary Omnibus Service' above the name of the railway. The buses, operated from Holloway Garage, worked from Euston - where they had a spacious covered terminal under the elegant arches of the old arrival-side carriage way to Moorgate Underground station stopping only outside the intermediate Underground stations on the way.

Then from January 1, 1923 this auxiliary omnibus service was extended from Moorgate to Clapham Common, on weekdays only with a three minute headway as before.The through fare was sixpence. A further thirty B-type were painted in the handsome blue livery and all forty six were then allotted to Putney Bridge and Putney (Chelverton Road) Garages. On November 29, 1923 the remaining section of the railway, from Moorgate to Clapham Common was closed for rebuilding and from this date the auxiliary omnibus service was intensified.

The service now worked daily between Moorgate and Clapham Common at one-minute intervals, and for this twenty-seven more B-type were put on from other garages, of which at least twenty remained in their red livery with only a small blue board screwed over the name 'General' on the sides with the railway's name. These buses, stopping as they did only outside Underground stations, travelled fast between stops and were a delight to ride on, and they were well patronised by regular travellers. All were withdrawn on June 11, 1924 the L.G.O.C. putting on Route 5B for the service using NS-type buses until the railway re-opened on December 1, 1924.

During the 1922 summer season the L.G.O.C. was running a publicity campaign urging travel in "London's Country" with posters, and introduced the polished aluminium figure of a rabbit on the radiator-caps of all the buses on country routes, and these were carried by many both double and single-deck B-type.

Sixteen B-type were loaned to the City and South London Railway to provide an omnibus service between the railway stations while this Underground line was being rebuilt. B 665 in a blue livery is operating from Holloway garage.

The B-type now began to take more and more a back seat as it were giving way on most inner-London services to the new buses being introduced. By 1921 there were 1,050 K-type in use, followed by 840 of the larger, fifty-four seat S-type and in 1923 by the more luxurious NS-type with its low frame and one-step entrance, of which by 1925 there were 1,750 in service, many of them being subsequently fitted with covered tops.

Similarly too in the single-deck field the B-type gradually gave way to later types if not so rapidly, the replacements being first the S-type thirty-seater in 1922-23 and then, in the summer of 1925 the twenty-four seat K-type. Although many of these new buses were operated on entirely new routes, it was the K-type, on solid or pneumatic tyres, which eventually displaced the B-type on the Muswell Hill and other single-decker routes.

No B-type bus, double or single-deck, ever ran on pneumatic tyres in London but four were rebuilt as nineteen-seater charabancs in July 1922 and were then so fitted. The tyres were of the high-pressure type, smaller in section than the so-called "giant pneumatic" used later on buses. The four converted were B1263, B1588, B2063 and B1064, which were fitted with Daimler engines and renumbered C1-C4. The first three were allocated to 'National' at Watford for private hire and C4 was retained by 'General' for the same purpose. Another four charabancs of the same type were licensed in May and June 1923; these had been B307, B369, B1485 and B1621 and now became C7 - C10 and re-registered as NK 5672/3, 5803/4, C5 and C6 were twenty-seat single-deck 'National' buses for one-man operation.

B 5067 one of the 26-seater operating on the Forest Hill and Chislehurst - 109 route has an aluminion rabbit on the radiator cap indicating it is on a country route. It is seen outside Nunhead garage.

By 1924 the only bus-company name seen on the sides of B-type buses other than the 'Metropolitan' or 'General' was that of 'Southern'. The 'Associated' company had been wound up at the end of the War and its fleet absorbed into 'General' and between September 1922 and September 1923 all the 238 'Metropolitan' B-type followed. They were transferred to 'General' as they came in for annual overhaul, being replaced in the Tramway's fleet by K- and S-type. The 'Gearless' were also withdrawn but were not replaced by other types as that company had sold out to the L.G.O.C. in 1922, though the 'Southern' eventually received K- and S-type replacement buses.

A special vehicle in use at this period (and also on pneumatic tyres) was B2758 which, was converted in 1922 into a mobile cinema unit, being basically a closed van but with large extensions at the rear which could be folded outwards to give a darkened space for daylight screening of films. This was occasionally used in public but it was mainly for showing of training and safety films at the garages, and the radiator was adorned for good measure with the metal rabbit symbol. It was sold off as a complete unit in 1925.

Although many of the London bus routes had progressed from B- to K-type and thence on to S- or NS-type,several continued to be worked by B-type up to 1923 or 1924, only to be replaced directly by new NS-type buses. Noted in this respect were for instance the Routes 1, 49 and 68. Some routes which had been allocated newer types even reverted to B-type at times, one example of this being Route 78 - operated entirely by K-type in 1921, but from late 1922 up to 1924 back to B-type.

Four B-type were rebuilt in July 1922 as 19-seat charabancs and fitted with pneumatic tyres. C 1-3 were operated by National but C 4 formerly B 1064 was retained by L.G.O.C. for Private Hire work.

The gradual withdrawal of the B-type double-deckers can however be seen from the numbers still licensed each year. The number of B-type double-deckers still licensed at the end of 1922 was 1,238, then 1,061 in 1923, 518 in 1924 and 447 in 1925. Considerable use was still made of the withdrawn buses however, and between the end of March and early May 1925 fifty selected B-type double-deck buses were, overhauled and transferred to the Private Hire Department. They were kept in very clean condition and embellished with white paint on the side of the tyres and were frequently seen in use. B340, already selected the previous year for eventual preservation, was one of these. These of this fleet, B319, 1084 and 1286 were sold to Great Yarmouth Corporation in June 1925, being replaced by three others.

At the end of the summer season on September 30, 1925, twenty five were withdrawn, followed by the others before the end of that year. Then in December 1925 ten of these buses were sent - on loan - to Liverpool to work for the Waterloo and Crosby Motor Services, who bought five of them B 529, 1685, 2169, 2604 and 4957 the others B 479, 536, 1306, 1374 and 2643 were returned during 1926. Also in 1925 ten were loaned (though not this time from the Private Hire fleet) to Birmingham City Transport Authority for temporary service on an Outer Circle route, pending the delivery of new A.E.C.buses. The ten which retained their red livery were B 465, 611, 1150, 1561 1734, 2295, 2456, 2531 4971 and 5091. In November 1925 B 1734 was returned and replaced by B104 and all were handed back within a few months.

Five of the C-type 19 seat charabancs operated by National were sold to an operator in Jersey where this picture of C9 was taken.

B 2758 was in 1922 converted into a mobile cinema unit, fitted with pneumatic tyres and given the metal rabbit symbol.

The conductor of B 1995 is busy changing the route board of this 73 bus at Hammersmith before returning to Stoke Newington. It is followed by a 9 going to Barnes.

B 48 is caught in a flooded road in Kingston when on the way to Putney Bridge Stataion.

No route boards were carried on the sides of the B-type in 1925 when this pictue of B 21 was taken at Wandsworth Common on route 67A.

B 5108 seen at the London Bridge terminus of route 18 is one of the buses new in 1919 with the later 'three panel' body and so the running number, AC 23 has been moved to the chassis frame.

The driver of B 943 checks the radiator while it is standing outside the 'Lord Nelson' at Millwall Docks. It has a new style of front route number box as used on the K-types.

Then on December 31, 1925 a further 233 B-type double-deck buses were withdrawn and these, together with the other unlicensed buses, appear to have been stored at Chiswick Works. Some were sold complete, others as scrap, and the worn-out bodies were tipped on to the ground and burned.

CHAPTER 10

THE LAST B-TYPE IN SERVICE AND THE GENERAL STRIKE
G. J. Robbins

At the beginning of 1926 a total of 214 B-type double-deck buses were licensed for public service, including six for 'Southern' but this much reduced fleet was spread among twenty-five garages in numbers varying from twenty at Turnham Green to a mere one a piece at Loughton and Hanwell; their purpose may have been partly to provide spare buses in the event of breakdowns. However, there was yet one more important role the B-type was to play in meeting Londoners' needs, and this was brought about by the General Strike in 1926.

The General Strike began at midnight on May 3, 1926 when the Trades Union Congress called out its members in all industries. The railways and the majority of the bus and tram systems throughout the country came to a standstill and the public looked on with wonder but made valiant efforts to get to work. Volunteers offered to run bus, tram, and train services and the companies accepted them and hoped for the best. The L.G.O.C., faced with the complete suspension of its services, prepared an emergency plan and withdrew all its 214 licensed B-type from their garages and concentrated them at Chiswick.

At the Works they were protected by Army personnel from interference, and it was no doubt considered that these vehicles, which had by now little book-value, could be used with impunity and entrusted to unskilled volunteer drivers to provide a public service. The volunteers came from all walks of life and included many undergraduates. Since there was some danger of the buses being attacked by the strikers, each bus carried a policemen or special constable who sat beside the driver, the B-type bus with its full width driving seat being easily able to carry two or even three abreast. As an added precaution against interference, barbed wire was draped over the bonnets. A Strike Centre was set up at Chiswick, and improvised depots for buses and fuel were established in the Royal Parks and were guarded by soldiers with fixed bayonets.

Four circular bus routes were devised, to be operated from Chiswick using B-type buses. All had special running numbers from A-1 upwards, and the routes were as follows:

Circular Route 1 (86 Buses) Ealing, Notting Hill Gate, Kensington, Ealing

The London B-Type Motor Omnibus

Circular Route 3 (64 Buses) Chelsea, Notting Hill Gate, Camden Town, Charing Cross, Chelsea

Circular Route 4 (78 Buses) Harlesden, Tottenham Court Road, Bank, Marble Arch, Harlesden

Circular Route 5 (84 Buses) Hendon, St.John's Wood, Victoria Station, Hendon

Possibly a Circular Route No.2 was planned but not implemented. In order to make these services of maximum use to the public as well as to assist the volunteer conductors a minimum fare of threepence was set. No.1 Route began on May 5, No.5 on May 6, No.3 on May 7, and sufficient volunteers were available by Saturday May 8 to start Route No.4.

B-type buses ran the whole of Routes 1 and 5, but as there were not enough licensed ones available some K-, S- and NS-types were used to complete the quota for the other routes. Sunday was a rest day but on Monday May 10 the Cricklewood Garage was reopened and four normal bus routes were operated by volunteers using K-, S- and NS-type buses.

It is worth recording that the L.G.O.C. were scrupulous about using only buses that were licensed even in the emergency. In contrast many private operators used unlicensed buses, lorries and even steam waggons for their improvised passenger services. The writer travelled to work early in the strike on one of these lorries but on the other days by a similar volunteer operated service by Thomas Tillings's buses.

A change was made on May 11 when the Circular Routes were withdrawn and the standard Routes 11, 18, 27, 33 and 184 operated by B-type buses from Chiswick. On the next day, the last of the Strike, additional buses from Chiswick ran on Routes 14, 49 and 73. Though the Strike was called off that day the reduced services continued for two days more, but normal working on all services was resumed by May 15.

Undoubtedly the B-type buses, many of them fifteen years old,had carried the main part of the burden, and to have rendered this last service so well to the people of London was truly remarkable.

The Editor of the 'Commercial Motor' pointed out the ingenuity shown by transport operators when he wrote:

"Road transport was the rock upon which the big stick was broken. The individual in road transport proved to be an unassailable force. He took his buses, his coaches, his vans, his lorries, and with merely a chalked inscription or a paper label, he constituted a new transport system"

As the London bus services returned to normal, the B-type were returned to the various garages whence they had come, but for some it was only a brief sojourn as, beginning in June 1926, they were gradually withdrawn and their licences cancelled. 158 were withdrawn in 1926 and the remaining 58 in 1927. Although some were still licensed for passenger service up to August 1927 (the very last were in fact six of the former 'Southern' buses B2271, B2286, B2289, B2290, B2291 and B2294) it is not easy to determine the actual last operation of B-type

Amongst the number of B-type relicenced for use during the General Strike in May 1926 was B 2271 still showing its SOUTHERN fleet name.

Barbed wire and a policeman protected B 5006 when it reached Central London on Circular route number 5 during the strike.

double-deckers on public service. The writer recalls riding on B1910 on May 28,1926 between Westminster and Dulwich, the bus bearing duty number 'S-12' on Route 112B, then normally operated by K-type, and there was another ride the next day on B4903 on the same duty.

Some of the last scheduled operations were those of nineteen from Leyton Garage on Route 22 on July 27, and of six from Hounslow Garage on Route 97 on August 24, 1926. It may be that the very last in service were two or three on Route 28 from Battersea Garage and some from Chalk Farm and Nunhead Garages on Route 63, last seen on October 12, 1926.

The few remaining licensed B-type double-deckers were no doubt kept as spares at various garages and only used as need arose in the first six months of 1927. Twenty of the last to be withdrawn, in the summer of 1927, were taken out of service from Merton Garage.

Meanwhile the withdrawal of the twenty - and twenty-six-seat single-deck B-type had commenced in 1925, the first being some surplus vehicles and then the twelve which had been on loan to Thomas Tilling, which had been replaced by new Tilling-Stevens 'TS-7' type buses. At the beginning of 1926 a total of 85 B-type single-deckers were licensed and during the next twenty two months these were gradually replaced by new single-deck K-type. The last scheduled B-type operations in April 1927 were of five twenty-seaters on Route 41 and one on Route 110, one twenty-six-seater still in use on Route 104, and two more from Sidcup Garage on Route 109. The last to be withdrawn on October 20, 1927, were one twenty-seater B442 and four twenty-six-seaters B122, B925, B5032 and B5065.

It is worthy of note that the very last operation of B-type buses in London (though not in this instance for fare-paying passengers) was that on behalf of the Associated Equipment Company which had built them. In 1927 the A.E.C. having outgrown its Walthamstow works had opened new works at Southall to which for a while they had to provide daily transport for their workers from their homes still in East London. For this a fleet of twenty four B-type double-deckers was obtained from Chiswick twelve in February 1927 and the rest in April and May the same year. Not being any longer, in this duty, subject to the stringent police regulations, they were promptly fitted with Cape-cart type hoods to the upper deck for protection against rain and transverse seats inside, increasing total seating capacity to forty. All but three of this small fleet came from the buses which had still been licensed in 1926 and were thus in good running order, as also was B45, formerly retained for occasional display on ceremonial parades and now giving a last service to its builders.

These buses were repainted in dark blue and bore the factory's name, and letters of the alphabet for identification. About 1,200 workers had to be transported twice daily, involving three overlapping shifts plus the office staff, and the journey required from one to one-and-a-half hours according to the traffic conditions. It was a miniature transport concern of its own and had to be closely timed.

This B-type fleet was reduced to twenty after August 1927 when two massive 104-seat LS-type six-wheelers, experimental vehicles never licensed for public service, were put into use on this work,which also provided a long-term realistic test for the two types of engine that were being tried out. The service then gradually declined as more workers moved house but many B-type continued in service

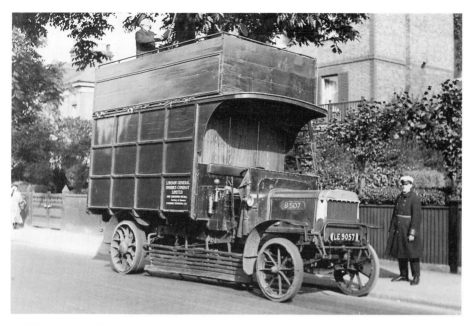

B 507 was specially adapted for trimming trees along London's bus roads.

throughout 1928 and the last were withdrawn in March 1929.

Among the departments transferred to Chiswick Works, as described previously, was the Driving School, and for this a small fleet of B-type buses was retained including one for skid-control practice. Many B-type chassis were retained for use as service vehicles, some of which had always been lorries while others were converted from buses. These included general service lorries as well as the panel bodied ticket-vans. Four B-type buses had been converted as long ago as 1916 into sludge-tanks with gulley-emptying gear - B1302, B1319, B1514, and B1523 - and to these B1809 was added in 1923, all five remaining in use till June 1928 when the bodies were transferred to new A.E.C. chassis and the B-type scrapped.

Another special vehicle was B2822, whose chassis had been shortened to enable a tipping body to be fitted. A familiar sight in the leafier parts of London was B507, adapted for trimming trees. The lower deck windows were boarded up, the top deck seats removed and a hatchway cut in the floor to absorb the lopped greenery. In 1927, B507 was fitted with a larger body specially designed for the job, and it was sold as a complete unit in 1928.

During the period of large-scale-production of K-type, Chiswick kept a small fleet of bare B-type chassis to bring new bodies from the outside builders and to carry them round inside the works; these were not registered, and carried the letters 'CP' on their bonnets instead of chassis numbers, but one of these is known to have been B2056.

Some of the special B-type vehicles kept at Chiswick Works proved to have the longest life of all. These included the nine box-vans dating from-war days - six for the Ticket Department - B 703, 724, 730, 1021, 1397 and 1533 and three for the

Advertising Department - B1017, B1018 and B2480. In 1923 B1018 had been scrapped but two more ticket-vans were added - B1012 in 1922 and B2251 in 1923 - and finally this fleet was made up to twelve by the addition of B1116 and B1736 in 1925, all these being conversions from double-deckers. All twelve were withdrawn in June 1928 and replaced by S-type vans similarly converted from double-deck buses, and the B-type were sold a month or two later.

Several double-deck buses were long kept for training duties - B5015 was in use for this late in 1927 and frequently went out on the road, while others were B2285 and B2316, which lasted to November 1930 before being scrapped.

Another long-lived service unit was B2745 which had been converted in 1921 into a mobile water-tank and tool-carrier and was thereafter often seen at functions such as the Wembley Cup Finals, where it kept a fleet of boiling NS-type buses supplied with water. It lasted in this form till May 1930 (when its body was put on a newer chassis) and it was then fitted with a double-deck body for further use in the Training School.

Two lorries and one chassis actually out-lasted the L.G.O.C. and passed to the London Passenger Transport Board. These were B4880 and B4881. allocated from the beginning to the London Electric-Railway and in use until October 1934, and last of all the chassis of B2134 which, built in 1912, thus achieved twenty-four years of work, being in use at Earls Court as a mobile generator until the beginning of 1936.

It is appropriate to conclude this chapter with a summary of the total number of B-type vehicles used by the L.G.O.C. and its associated concerns, and the A.E.C. for its L.G.O.C. work. It should be noted that B4865 and B4867 were lorries retained by the A.E.C. and B4880 - B4882 lorries supplied to the London Electric Railway in 1918, and also that B5133 and B5134, were not originally built as B-type but were the former buses X39 and X58 later fitted with lorry bodies and subsequently with B-type engines, upon which they were renumbered. Totals are given for two periods - that of 1910-1914 and again that of 1915-1919, and are as under:

B1-B2825 (less direct sales)	2,809	2,344*
B2826-B2859 (certain numbers only)	13	17
B3163-B3168	6	-
B3474-B3503-	-	30
B3706-B3774 (certain numbers only)	-	7
B3805-B3816 (certain numbers only)	-	6
B4865-B5134	-	267
B6865-B6889	-	25
	2,828	2,696

*i.e. less those which did not return from war to the L.G.O.C.

In addition to the eleven direct sales mentioned above five buses B 2814, 2818, 2820, 2823 and 2824 although delivered to the LGOC in August 1914 were handed back to the AEC and their registrations used up later.

CHAPTER 11

IN THE SERVICE OF OTHER OPERATORS
J. B. Atkinson

So robustly built and well maintained was the 'General' B-type fleet that the buses were in considerable demand when they were first offered for sale, whether by the Company from 1920 on or by Army Disposals a year earlier even though they might by then be up to ten years old.

When the War ended the Government had a very large number of surplus motor vehicles of all types for disposal including B-type as buses, lorries, ambulances or bare chassis, and these were disposed of by periodic auctions held at Slough from 1919 onwards.

As already noted, the L.G.O.C. itself had bought back some 396 of the vehicles it had lost at the beginning of the War (these in addition to the 103 obtained from the Government in 1915 and 1916) but not many of these were suitable for service as standard buses, most becoming 'Traffic Emergency Buses' or lorries or being dismantled for spares.

While most of the B-type chassis offered at Slough had come from the direct A.E.C. production for the War Department, several hundred would have been ex-L.G.O.C. buses, but unfortunately very few details are known of these. This is because they had mostly by then lost their identity and were in many cases re-registered by the buyers in the area in which they were going to work.

About half of those known became lorries, many serving for a further ten or more years, and spare parts from dismantled or incomplete chassis continued to be sold at Slough up to 1926. A handful of buses were sold out of war service while still overseas, where the end of the fighting had found them unneeded and not worth the cost of shipping home. Thus several were to be seen in civilian use in Athens and Thessalanike around 1919, adapted to unfamiliar Mediterranean sunshine with fringed cloth canopies over the top deck.

Out of some forty ex-L.G.O.C. B-type bought direct as war surplus whose history is known (and this is certainly only a small proportion of the total) eighteen are known to have re-entered passenger service. Of double-deck buses, Progressive Motors of Wellingborough bought B121 and B2708 (they later bought more from the L.G.O.C. when available), Plymouth Corporation bought B919, Adams of Balcombe B2206, London & Essex Motors of Ilford B2322, while the Laindon & District Motor Service bought the chassis of B214 and fitted it with an ex-National Steam Car body from that company's withdrawn fleet in 1919. C. Wayman of Waltham Abbey had B 1300 and fitted it with a single-deck body which was re-registered HK 9496. It was operated on a route between Waltham Cross and Waltham Abbey from a garage in High Bridge Street the route later being numbered 306. Both route and garage passed to National in 1926.

The twenty-seat single-deckers which had served as ambulances throughout the War and were probably therefore kept in good condition were evidently in great demand. Four went into further ambulance service with the Royal Navy and were stationed at Chatham, and Devonport. They were B 2680, 2681, 2684 and 2698. Six went into passenger service. These were B2679 and B2682 for Billesden of Leicester, B2683 for the Ministry of Munitions at Chepstow, B2688 for Clements of Workington, B2690 to Higgs & Waller of Melbourne who re-sold it to Barton Brothers, Beeston, and one - number unknown - to Central Motor Company of Barry, who bought it from War Disposals in 1919 and registered it as L 6339, using it till 1921. Four other chassis were adapted as charabancs - B1905 for Clements of Poplar, B2697 for Leeman of Waltham Abbey, B2722 for Markham of Laindon, and B2772 for Carey of New Romney - B816 for Parsons of Winterslow another charabanc and B1511 a lorry for the Direct Coal Supply Company of Thatcham.

Many were sold as lorries or only as chassis converted into lorries and these included a fleet of six to one operator, Brock in North London who had B 590, 683, 861, 995, 1405 & 2474. Others whose chassis numbers are not known were bought by Ashbys Ltd, and the Barnet Gas Company. The original registration numbers of all these chassis had been cancelled and so those mentioned had become B 121, DO 2213, B 919, CO 2701, B 2206, XA 9121, B 2322, HK 9745, B 214, HK 9421, B 2679, XB 8297, B 2682, XA 9198, B 2685, LY 9329, B 2688, MC 9870, B 2697, XA 9201, B 2704, XB 9724, B 2772. KE 2126, B 1405, XA 9127, B 683, LY 9322, B 861, XA 9757, B 995, XB 8788,

Turning now to sales by the L.G.O.C. itself a good deal of information has survived. The 'General' had no buses available for disposal until July 1920, when two double-deckers, B1575 and B1645, were sold to Barton Bros. of Beeston who already had B2690 and later bought B2305 and B2687. Twenty two more were sold early in October and though most of these went to dealers, three were bought by Great Yarmouth Corporation - B235, B647, and B1939 - and four by the Guernsey Railway Company - B630, B1183, B1275 and B1743. Other sales in 1920 were of three to Westcliff-on-Sea - B92, B200, and B1689 - four to the Economic Building Corporation - B962, B1493, B1873, and B1897 - and two apiece to Robinson of Scarborough - B1833 and B1842 and Thomas White of Cardiff - B488 and B759. Single sales were B198 to Ferguson of Belfast, B204 to Torquay Tramways, with registration TA 1803. B1655 to Worthmore Motors and B1882 to Peric Motors of Edinburgh who later acquired several more.

In June 1920 the L.G.O.C. loaned to the National Omnibus & Transport Company twenty type 7 buses, ten, B 4979, 4984, 4990, 5039, 5041, 5070, 5087, 5111, 5116, were for use in Chelmsford or Colchester whilst the other ten B 4929, 4939, 4947, 4980, 4981, 4996, 5076, 5077, 5082, 5117 in the Bedford area. Two of them B 4990 and 4979 were sold to National in December 1920 and then numbered 2101 and 2108 in the National fleet, replacing the B-type number. The other eighteen were sold to National in February 1922 when they were numbered 2139 - 2156 consecutively.

Over the next four years another 76 complete buses were sold by the L.G.O.C.

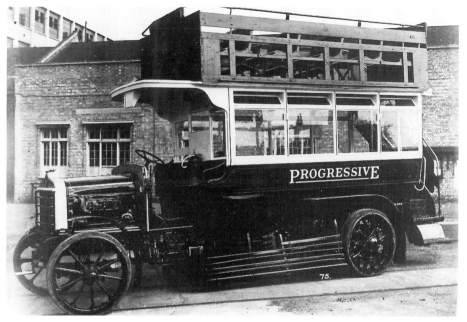

B 4873 was one of fourteen buses sold to Progressive Motor Services of Wellingborough in 1921.

One of the 26-seat single decks, number not known, went to Central Motor Company of Barry in South Wales.

to services with which the Company desired to co-operate or to those sufficiently remote from London to offer no threat of competition. The price was still quite high - around four hundred pounds (considerably more than the buses had originally cost) and at the same time the well built bodies were also in considerable demand.

Some hundreds of spare B-type bodies were sold in early post-war years, later to be seen in many places and mounted on many types of chassis.

By 1921 more buses were available for sale and Birkenhead Tramways bought several, two of which are known to have been B2026 and B2414 which lasted to 1925 and 1928 respectively. Two provincial operators built small fleets in this way; Progressive Motor Services of Wellingborough, which had earlier bought two buses direct from war surplus stocks as already mentioned now bought a further fourteen from the L.G.O.C. These were B 483 (DO 3119), B 527, (DO 2149), 597, 660 (DO 1527), 709, 747, 1145, 1166 (DO 2452), 1287, 2135, 2738, 4871 (DO 2958), 4872 (DO 2959), 4873 (DO 2960. New registrations where known shown in brackets. Progressive Motor Services had been formed in 1919 and in 1920 operated in Boston as well and later in Scunthorpe. Eleven of these B-type were sold to J. C. Robb of Outwell.

Similarly Peric Motors of Edinburgh after their experience with B 1882 obtained from Slough in 1920 bought eight more from the L.G.O.C., six of them being single-deckers B 443, 2857, 3486, 3488, 3501 & 4877 and double-decks B 853 and 1601. Other sales in 1921 were of B1615 and B1884 to Moon's Garages, B355 (a single-decker) to Worthmore Motor Services, B1629 to Devon General and B2766 to West Hartlepool Tramways who later converted it into a tower-waggon. It is also recorded that B1391 was presented to the Sulgrave Institution.

By 1922 the 'General' K- and S-type buses were rapidly coming into service and so more B-type could be made available for sale. At the same time however the Company was becoming understandably sensitive to the inroads of independent bus operators in London, and had no wish to be plagued by its own good buses in other operators' hands.

For this reason a condition of sale advertised was that the buses sold might not be operated within thirty miles of London. By now too the price had fallen sometimes to as low as a hundred pounds for a complete bus; that this was still a good price however is shown by the fact that the Tilling TTA-type petrol-electric bus was being sold complete at this period for as little as twenty five pounds.

In February 1922 another twenty four more B-type buses were sold to National Omnibus Company being the older or 'type 3' vehicles. Six B 269, 997, 1658, 2202, 2494, 2754 went to Colchester, three B 904, 1583, 1938 to Bedford but the other sixteen were sent to the West of England where National were setting up branches, so nine B 1171, 1204, 1226, 1249, 1293, 1631, 1686, 2513 and 2737 were sent to Stroud and Trowbridge and six to Taunton and Yeovil. Two were double deck B 1048 and 1056 and four single-deck B 1730, 1815, 1900, 2390. Lastly B 1053 sold as a chassis was rebodied as a 20-seat single-deck and registered as YA 2142 for use at Taunton. These twenty five buses were numbered into the National fleet as 2114 - 2138.

Another sale this year was that of B 1616 and B 2558 to Road Motors of Luton. So good was the reputation of the B-type that four B 1245, 1380, 1863 & 2665 were shipped to Australia in May and September 1922.They went to G.Mason who

B 5117 was one of the buses loaned to National Omnibus & Transport Company by the
L.G.O.C. in 1920 but purchased two years later when it was given the number 2156 by
National. It was allocated to Bedford garage.

worked a country bus service with them starting from Spencer Street, Melbourne,
and for sentimental reasons restored the name 'General' to his buses. They must
have stood up well to bad roads as in the following year he bought no less than
twenty five more chassis while another Australian bus operator had five B-type
shipped out in May 1923, these were B 638, 1764, 1949, 1958, 2147. Incredibly,
one of the Australian consignment remained in service on an outlying farm for fifty
years more, the owner driving it into North Melbourne to offer in part-exchange
1972.

Two sales in 1923 produced interesting experimental vehicles. B2435 was
bought by the coachbuilding firm, Strachan & Brown of Kensington who built their
own single-deck body on it and exhibited it outside the Commercial Motor
Exhibition at Olympia that year. B1337 was bought by F. H. Beck of Broadstairs
who patented and demonstrated a folding cloth hood for the top deck and used the
bus, carrying the name "allweather", for demonstration purposes in London during
March 1923. The hood was claimed to be a one-man-operated affair capable of
being erected by the conductor unaided, and it could be folded up out of use over
the driver's canopy.

Around this time the L.G.O.C. stated to the press that it was being "inundated
with suggestions for fitting some form of allweather covering to the tops of motor
buses but was not in a position to deal with suggestions of this nature until the new
NS-type bus had made its appearance. That they had studied B1337 fairly carefully
however is suggested by the fact that in March 1924 one B-type double-decker was

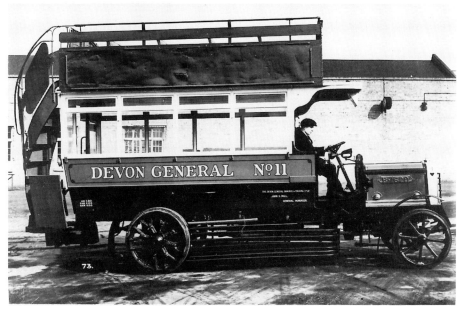

Although Devon General had many A.E.C. buses B 1629 was the only B-type operated.

fitted with a rather similar type of folding cloth hood for tilting tests at Chiswick Works.The writer saw it only once, on March 15, and it was kept carefully out of sight in the works and unpublicised to avoid raising false hopes of better protection in the public mind.

By now there were relatively few sales of B-type as buses, and the price asked was very low. The firm of J. Blake was now offering the double-deckers for £85, which included their own commission, and the L.G.O.C. probably preferred to hire them out when needed, as they did to both Birmingham and Liverpool transport undertakings. Another factor may have been the growing introduction of covered top buses in the provinces (where there was nothing like the official opposition that London suffered in this respect) which would reduce the demand for the more spartan older type of bus.

There were however still some bus sales and in 1923 these included three to Cornwall Enterprise Motors - B470, B539 and B1489 - and four to Hastings of Pimbury - B205, B1260, B1985 and B2129 - who subsequently exported some or all of them to Brussels. Five more were sold to J. C. Robb of Wisbech to work Outwell Motor Services, these were B 390, 478, 552, and 908 in 1923 and 1104 in 1924. B1329 went to Laindon & District Services which already had war-surplus B214 in service in the Billericay area.

In 1924 B6872 was bought by F. Egginton of Walthamstow, and in 1925 there were still a few sales of complete buses, such as the Waterloo and Crosby Motors' purchase of five (out of the ten it had hired temporarily as earlier described) for further use. The Isle of Thanet Tramways bought two single-deckers B2221 and

B 1245 was one of four buses shipped to Australia in May 1922 for G. Mason who ran a country route from Melbourne.

An attempt was made to put a roof on this B-type which went to Greece.

B3474, and Central Omnibus Services of Norwich bought B1139. Also a double-decker was sold to a firm in Buenos Aires, but its number is not known.

Still in 1925, Great Yarmouth Corporation Tramways bought B319, B1084 and B1286, all to replace the three B-type they had bought five years earlier, which must have given very good service. They also bought B2631 for spares and kept it to as late as May 1935.

By 1926 most of the sales were of chassis or lorries, but a handful were still sold as double-deckers. Portsmouth Corporation bought B2017, only using it till the following year but keeping it in store, by then a single-decker and in derelict condition up to 1932. Temple Fortune Motors of Golders Green had B1469 which the writer saw in their yard still painted red and apparently for re-sale. One of the large twenty-six-seat single-deckers was bought by Premier Motors of Keighley - B5121.

In 1927 at least one double-decker was sold - B5010 to Downing Bros. of Greenwich - and two of the pneumatic-tyred charabancs were sold to Pope of Hockcliffe - C1 formerly B1263 and C3 formerly B2063 C7 - 10 were sold to an operator in Jersey. Perhaps on of the last sales of all of double-deckers may have been that of B387, noted by the writer running in London on March 7, 1928, painted grey overall but it is not known for whom it was destined.

A few sales remain to be noted, though the exact years of sale are not known. B1464 went to McArdle Motors of Dundalk, B2168 to the body-building firm of Hora who later shipped it to Cairo, B2455 to the Royal Ordnance Factory at Woolwich, and B6875 to Russell of Hounslow.

The B-type bus body tended of course to outlast its chassis, even as the bodies of earlier types had done, and could be seen in most unexpected spots in the country side in use as caravans, bungalows, toolsheds, greenhouses, chicken coops, club houses and shelters for many years. Those in better condition were sold for further passenger use in the provinces mounted on other chassis; the twenty sold to 'East Surrey' for mounting on A.E.C. Y-type chassis have already been noted and there were sales of bodies to at least five concerns already operating B-type buses - Barton Bros, United Automobile Services of Durham, Road Motors of Luton, Isle of Thanet Tramways and Portsmouth Corporation, which mounted one on a Thornycroft chassis in 1926 and later preserved it.

Other buyers of double-deck bodies from the L.G.O.C. were British Automobile Traction, Palladium Autocars, Devon Motor Transport, Tresillian Motors of Cardiff, Hadleigh and District Motor Services, and a bus operator in Thundersley.

By now the main use being made of B-type however was as lorries, particularly on such work as food and coal delivery and household removals on which long mileages were not involved. Most were one-man concerns, but there were a few small fleets. Henry Evans & Co. had at least four, and Charrington Gardner Locket & Co. bought at least five chassis, though probably for re-sale.

Three lorries were adapted to be rather spartan buses; thus B60 was modified by Slough & District Motor Services to a "lorry-bus" and, painted a bright pink, used for summer holiday tours in the Thames Valley, and B2478 - also in - Slough - was operated by the firm of Weaver in a similar way, while B2704, sold as a lorry to Goss of Shadwell, emerged as a "lorry-bus" or single-decker of some kind for use by the St.Helens Cooperative Society.

After being sold B 1743 became number 3 in the fleet of Guernsey Railway Company.

B 2824 which was one of the five buses that had been handed back to the AEC in 1914 was disposed of after the war to J. E. Moore of Wigan and registered as a lorry CX 3818.

A notable group of lorries were also the "tower-waggons" of the Associated Tramway Companies, to whom B-type chassis were sold over the years between 1920 and 1928. With the disappearance of the tram they are almost forgotten but they were a most necessary piece of equipment. They had a wooden latticework tower mounted on the frame and a rotating platform at the top which could be raised and lowered by hand and swung out over the side enabling work to be done on overhead wires without interrupting the passing of tramcars. One such apparatus, beautifully restored, has been preserved in a Leicester museum mounted on a Leyland chassis.

All three associated tramway systems in London used such vehicles, replacing earlier horse-drawn appliances, and they seem to have transferred the fleet among one another to a certain extent, since units bought by one tramway might eventually be sold off by another one.

The first for conversion, B2678 was sold to the 'M.E.T' in 1920 followed by four more - B345, B912, B2584 and B4875 - in 1921. The London United Tramways bought B239 and B808 in 1922 and in the following year the 'M.E.T' bought three more - B177, B941 and B2501 - and the L.U.T. one more - B171 - while 'Southmet' bought B302. Latter on the 'M.E.T' bought still another five - B4959, B5043 and B5114 in 1926 and B1058 and B4870 in 1928, They were all sold between April an August 1930. At least one provincial tram-way system, that of West Hartlepool,

A B-type sold by Daimler to Rotherham Corporation Tramways is standing outside the Walthamstow works.

made a similar conversion on B2766, which they had bought in 1920 as a double-deck bus.

Two of Chiswick Works' specialised vehicles were sold off complete - B2758 the mobile cinema in 1925, and B507 the tree-trimmer in 1928. A few chassis were used at Chiswick up to the end of 1930, and the last disposal of all was not until London 'Transport days in 1936.

The London B-type bus thus served out its last years in humbler duties, but fortunately a few examples have been preserved. The idea that it is worth while to cherish the evidence of the craftsmanship upon which British industry has been built up has, if slowly, taken root, and in an age which has only recently woken up to the importance of preserving outstanding machines of its industrial heritage, four B-type buses, looking more and more strange to each succeeding generation, have survived as reminders.

CHAPTER 12

THE PRESERVED BUSES
J. B. Atkinson

Three B-type buses, all double-deckers, have been preserved - B43, B214 and B340 - the first two having served overseas during the First World War.

B43 was built in 1911 and initially allocated to Clay Hall Garage. It was requisitioned in October 1914, driven to Avonmouth, shipped to Rouen and sent up with troops to St. Omer, all so hurriedly that there was no time to paint it green and it shone red and white and proclaimed the virtues of soap and whiskey most unsuitably at the front. It was then mustered in the 90th. Company of the Army Service Corps, painted a decent dark green, and had its windows boarded up, and in this form it served for nearly five years.

The bus was returned in 1919 along with several hundreds of others, all battered badly, but the L.G.O.C. inspected it and deemed it worth repairing, overhauled the chassis and fitted it with a body out of store and put it on the road as a "Traffic Emergency Bus" to work on Route 8.

In 1920 there was a call for a motor bus that had served in the War to take a party of ex-servicemen to be inspected by King George V, and B43 was chosen and driven into Buckingham Palace on February 14. After this it was adorned with a shell above the dashboard and a figure of the legendary soldier "Ole Bill" on the radiator cap,and returned to Dalston Garage from which it worked on Routes 8 and 9 for several years more. When the time came for withdrawal a fresh body, in better condition, was fitted and the advertisements stripped, and the bus then presented to the Auxiliary Omnibus Companies Old Comrades Association. For the next fifteen years it was seen occasionally on the road for such events as Armistice Day anniversaries and British Legion pageants. It took part in the 1929 procession celebrating the centenary of the omnibus, During the second World War it was stored in various London Transport garages. Afterwards the Board continued to keep B43 in running order for special events and used it itself for a promotional tour of London to introduce the new "Roadmaster" bus in 1967. It also appeared in various rallies of historic vehicles, and was finally retired on May 5, 1970 when it was driven by ex-service veteran driver George Gwynne into the Imperial War Museum at Lambeth where it adds a touch of colour to the khaki of the tanks and guns that surround it. Alongside it stands a model of it in its Army colours and fittings.

B214 was built in 1911 and initially allocated to Turnham Green Garage, from which it had opened, on July 14, 1912, one of the first long country bus routes with

B 43, the bus chosen as a reminder of the excellent work done by the busmen and B-type buses during the 1914-18 war was at first retained in service and operated from Dalston garage on routes 8 and 9. Note the words 'Traffic Emergency Bus' behind the GENERAL fleet name.

which the L.G.O.C. was experimenting in that year, route 45 from Harlington to Staines. Taken out of service and sent overseas in 1914 it had its bus body taken off and replaced by a general type of lorry body, it was so damaged in service that when it was returned in 1919 as a bare chassis, the L.G.O.C. inspected it and decided that it was not worth their repurchasing. The chassis was therefore sold as scrap by the War Disposals Co; at Slough where several hundreds of similar chassis and engines were on sale.

Many enterprising ex-service men were at that time buying old chassis and fitting them up as lorries for small businesses and an Essex man named Hinton was somewhat more adventurous and decided to found a bus line. He therefore bought the chassis of B214 and drove it to Chelmsford, where at that time the "National" steam buses which were being withdrawn from London were being dismantled for scrap. Their bodies however were in fair condition and many were being re-used,and Hinton mounted one on his chassis. With his bus he founded the Laindon & District Motor Service, based on Grays Hill near Billericay. His venture prospered and he bought a complete B-type double-decker from the L.G.O.C. as soon as these were available. When the service closed down after his death the chassis and body remained many years in use as a toolshed, and it was on this chassis that parts from other dismantled B-type lorries were collected and eventually mounted. An engine was found on a long derelict B-type chassis in Northampton, wheels and front axle from a trailer that had been once a B-type bus in a quarry near Shepperton, a complete single-deck body in very good condition at Canvey, and

When withdrawn from service B 43, was fitted with another body and was used on special occasions, anniversaries or pagents. Eventually it was presented to the Imperial War Museum and is seen arriving at the Museum on May 5. 1970 driven by ex-service veteran driver George Gwynne.

assembly was done on a farm near Gloucester. The single-deck body, which had come off B5103, was clearly somewhat inappropriate (it had been built in 1921) so the body of a double-decker was found in a garden at Horsham this was mounted on the chassis and B214 was properly complete. The body was one sold to the "East Surrey" in 1912 (as the layers of paint revealed) and had been painted dark red all over - a practice the L.G.O.C. had given up by 1913 - so there was no doubt about its provenance. Top deck seats had to be made - for which scale drawings were offered by the Transport Board - and the back stairs built,and the vehicle was complete. posters were copied from old photographs (Schweppes, Dunlop, Pears and so on) and the many destination - and route-boards for Route 12 restored, and the large brass acetylene headlamp fitted and the restoration was completed having been done by relays of students and taken about fourteen years. B 214 eventually entered the Museum of the London Bus Preservation Club at Cobham Surrey in January 1980. It was subsequently sold to another enthusiast, David Goodey but in September 1990 it was sold again to a Dutch Motor Museum.

The story of B340 is less complex. Like the other two it had been built in 1911 (it was initially allocated to Middle Row Garage, in North Kensington) and in 1914 requisitioned for war service. This however was not overseas but in London where several buses were used for convalescent wounded and for various duties in connection with home defence. It was therefore kept in good condition and when the Government permitted the re-purchase of 108 buses to ease the travelling

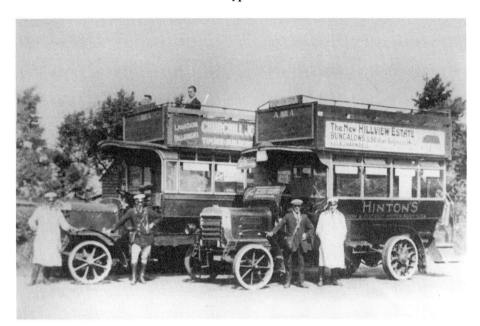

B 214 a with an ex-National Steam car body seen at Billericay in 1923 when in the fleet of Mr Hinton.

B214 after the restoration was completed in 1979.

Members of the Omnibus Society had an opportunity of travelling on B 340 also K 424 on the occasion of the Society's Sliver Jubilee on September 25. 1954. This interesting journey started from the Commercial Motor Show at Earls Court and finished at Waterloo Place off Pall Mall.

situation, especially that of thousands of munition factory workers, B340 was one of those chosen. It re-entered public service in 1916,at first carrying its war-time body but later this was changed for one of the newest type, many of which had been put in store in 1914. It was then allocated to Kingston Garage from which it worked for the next eight years.

With drawn in December 1924,it was selected for preservation and kept under dust covers in Chiswick Works. It was however kept in running order and was occasionally used on private hire work from 1925 onwards.

When in 1936 a typical London bus was wanted to take part in a parade for the golden jubilee of the City of Vancouver B340 - , was shipped from Surrey Docks to that city in February and returned in December of that year. In the second World War it was moved out from Chiswick and stored at Guildford from 1941 and moved to Reigate in 1946 and to the Museum of London Transport in 1960. Here it was repainted, stripped of advertisements and given the place of honour in the converted Clapham tram depot which housed both rail and road machines. When this museum closed it was moved in 1973 to Syon Park, this time a purely London Transport affair, and when this in turn was closed B340 was taken to Covent Garden in 1980 where it is currently on display at the head of a line of its 'General' successors.

Thus three 1911 buses are safely in museums and portray to succeeding generation somewhat Spartan conditions in which their forefathers rode to work and pleasure.

APPENDIX A

CHASSIS AND REGISTRATION NUMBERS, BODY, WAR SERVICE, FLEET AND (WHERE KNOWN) THE INITIAL GARAGE ALLOCATION

A great deal of information has to be condensed in this Appendix, and symbols are used as listed below. The garage of first allocation, where known, is shown by the code-letter (see Appendix B) and the last of the descriptive symbols given is the last known informations.

1 General symbols

c - used as chassis only
d - conversion to (-d,) or from (d-) double-deck bus
ch - charabanc
L - lorry, van, or special vehicle
sb - private-hire or experimental bus
ss - sixteen-seat single-decker
st - twenty seat single-decker
sx - twenty six seat single-decker
z - chassis sold direct to an outside buyer

2. War Department service

* - service for WD, home or overseas
r5 - repurchased 1915, restored to standard bus
r6 - ditto, 1916
r9 - ditto, 1919
re - repurchased 1919 and fitted with standard body ("red" emergency bus")
ke - repurchased 1919 and worked as substandard bus ("khaki emergency bus")
rx - repurchased 1919 but scrapped.
/59 - shows the last part of "PAD" number carried. There was a prefix "41/" for all vehicles, so this is not shown.

Appendix A

3. Allocation to fleets

AS - "Associated"
CN - "Central"
CS - "City & South London Railway"
ES - "East Surrey"
GL - "Gearless"
ME - "M.E.T " (later "Metropolitan")
ME(r)- -ditto - (replacement buses 1915-20)
MS - "Metropolitan Steam Omnibus Company"
NO - "National" (loaned buses only, not sales)
SN - "Southern"
AE - "Associated Equipment Company"

All allocations are to the General fleet unless otherwise shown by symbol.
Two successive symbols show allocation to successive fleets in turn.

Vehicles listed are double-deck buses unless otherwise shown.
The following examples will show interpretation of the symbols:-

"2476 LF9586 ME*AK" refers to a "M.E.T" double-decker before the War, allocated to Streatham Garage, went to WD and not returned.

"2477 LF9881 CN*r9 AH" - "Central" double-deckcr, allocated Kingston, war service with WD repurchased 1919, restored to standard bus.

"2478 LH8036 *L/172" - a "General" double-decker, war service with WD, repurchased 1919 and used as lorry numbered "41/172"

"2479 LF9588 ME AK" - "M.E.T" double-decker allocated Streatham, remained in service throughout the War.

"2480 LF8647 L/159" - lorry, did not go to WD service, numbered "41/159" after the War.

"2481 LH8117 L*r9" - lorry before the War, then War service, repurchased 1919, became standard double-deck bus.

1	LN4701	*r5	Y	51	LN4751	*L/187	Y
2	LN4702	*r5	Y	52	LN4752	*ke	Y
3	LN4703	*re	Y	53	LN4753	*ke	Y
4	LN4704	*	Y	54	LN4754	*re	Y
5	LN4705	*	Y	55	LN4755	*	Y
6	LN4706	*ke	Y	56	LN4756	*r5ME(r)	Y
7	LN4707	*ke	Y	57	LN4757	*	Y
8	LN4708	*	Y	58	LN4758	*ke	Y
9	LN4709	*re	Y	59	LN4759	*ke	Y
10	LN4710.	*rx	Y	60	LN4760	*L/176	Y
11	LN4711	*r5	Y	61	LN4761		W
12	LN4712	*	Y	62	LN4762	d-ss-sx-re	W
13	LN4713	*	Y	63	LN4763		W
14	LN4714	*ke	Y	64	LN4764		W
15	LN4715	*	Y	65	LN4765		W
16	LN4716	*	Y	66	LN4766		W
17	LN4717	*	Y	67	LN4767	ME(r)	W
18	LN4718	*r5ME(r)	Y	68	LN4768		W
19	LN4719	*ke	Y	69	LN4769	*r9	W
20	LN4720	*r5ME(r)	Y	70	LN4770		W
21	LN4721	*r5	Y	71	LN4771		W
22	LN4722	*r5ME(r)	Y	72	LN4772		W
23	LN4723	*ke	Y	73	LN4773		W
24	LN4724	*	Y	74	LN4774		W
25	LN4725	*	Y	75	LN5994	L*	
26	LN4726	*	Y	76	LN4776		W
27	LN4727	*	Y	77	LN4777		W
28	LN4728	*r5.	Y	78	LN4778		W
29	LN4729		Y	79	LN4779	d-ss-d re	W
30	LN4730	*	Y	80	LN4780		W
31	LN4731	*r5	Y	81	LN4781	ME(r)	W
32	LN4732.	*9	Y	82	LN4782	ME(r)	W
33	LN4733	*ke	Y	83	LN4783		W
34	LN4734	*re	Y	84	LN4784		W
35	LN4735	*r5	Y	85	LN4785		W
36	LN4736	*r9	Y	86	LN4786		W
37	LN4737	*ke	Y	87	LN4787		W
38	LN4738	*	Y	88	LN4788		W
39	LN4739	*	Y	89	LN4789		W
40	LN4740	*	Y	90	LN4790		W
41	LN4741	*	Y	91	LN4791		W
42	LN4742	*ke ES	Y	92	LN4792		W
43	LN4743	*ke	Y	93	LN4793		W
44	LN4744	*L/160	Y	94	LN4794		W
45	LN4745	*r5 ME(r)AE	Y	95	LN4795		W
46	LN4746	*r9	Y	96	LN4796		W
47	LN4747	*ke	Y	97	LN4797	*r5	W
48	LN4748	*r5	Y	98	LN4798		W
49	LN4749	*	Y	99	LN4799		W
50	LN4750	*	Y	100	LN4800		W

101	LN4801		W	151	LN4678		W
102	LN4802		W	152	LN4679		W
103	LN4803		W	153	LN4680		W
104	LN4804		W	154	LN4681		W
105	LN4805		W	155	LN4682		W
106	LN4806	*	W	156	LN4683		W
107	LN4807		W	157	LN4684	ke	W
108	LN4808	*ke	W	158	LN4685		W
109	LN4809		W	159	LN4686		W
110	LN4810	*r6	W	160	LN4687		W
111	LN4811		W	161	LN4688		W
112	LN4812		W	162	LN4689		W
113	LN4813	*	W	163	LN4690		W
114	LN5995	L*		164	LN4691		W
115	LN4815	*r5	W	165	LN4692		W
116	LN4816	*r5 ME(r)	W	166	LN4693		W
117	LN4817	*	W	167	LN4694		W
118	LN4818	*	W	168	LN4695		W
119	LN4819	*	W	169	LN4696		W
120	LN4820	*	W	170	LN4697		W
121	LN4821	*	W	171	LN4698		W
122	LN4822	*ke-sx	W	172	LN4699		W
123	LN4823	*r5 *ME(r)	W	173	LN4700		W
124	LN4775	*	W	174	LC3813		W
125	LN4814	*	W	175	LN5996	L-d	W
126	LN4657	*r5	W	176	LC3814		W
127	LN4658	*	W	177	LC3815		W
128	LN4659	*r5	W	178	LC3816		W
129	LN4660	*rx	W	179	LC3817		W
130	LN4661	*	W	180	LC3818		W
131	LN4662	*	W	181	LC3819	ke	W
132	LN4663	*	W	182	LC3820		W
133	LN4664	*	W	183	LC3821		W
134	LN4665	*	W	184	LC3822	CS	W
135	LN4666	*ke	W	185	LC3823		W
136	LN4667	*r5 ME(r)	W	186	LC3824		W
137	LN4668	*L/188	W	187	LC3825		W
138	LN4669	*r5 CS	W	188	LC3826		W
139	LN4670	*	W	189	LC3827		W
140	LN4671	*r5	W	190	LC3828		W
141	LN4672	*L/174	W	191	LC3829		W
142	LN243	*	W	192	LC3830		W
143	LN274	*ke-L/193	W	193	LC3831		V
144	LN349	*d-L/158	W	194	LC3832		V
145	LN318	*	W	195	LC3833		V
146	LN4673	*L/I 64	W	196	LC3834		V
147	LN4674	*	W	197	LC3835		V
148	LN4675	*	W	198	LC3836		V
149	LN4676		W	199	LC3837		V
150	LN4677	*	W	200	LC3838		V

201	LN5997	L-d	V	251	LA9839		V
202	LC3839		V	252	LA9840		V
203	LC3840		V	253	LA9841		V
204	LC3841		V	254	LA9842		V
205	LC3842	ME(r)	V	255	LA9843		V
206	LC3843	*	V	256	LA9844		V
207	LC3844		V	257	LA9845		V
208	LC3845		V	258	LA9846		V
209	LC3846		V	259	LA9847		V
210	LC3847		V	260	LA9848		V
211	LC3848		V	261	LA9849		V
212	LC3849		V	262	LA9850		V
213	LA9801	ME(r)	V	263	LA9851		V
214	LA9802	*	V	264	LA9852		V
215	LA9803		V	265	LA9853		V
216	LA9804	*	V	266	LA9854	ME(r)	V
217	LA9805	*ke	V	267	LA9855		V
218	LA9806		V	268	LA9856		V
219	LA9807	*	V	269	LA9857		V
220	LA9808	*	V	270	LA9858		V
221	LA9809	*r6 ME(r)	V	271	LA9859		V
222	LA9810	*	V	272	LA9860		V
223	LA9811	*r6	V	273	LA9861	CS	V
224	LA9812	*	V	274	LA9862		V
225	LA9813	*re	V	275	LA9863		V
226	LA9814	*	V	276	LA9864		V
227	LA9815		V	277	LA9865		V
228	LA9816	*	V	278	LA9866		V
229	LA9817		V	279	LA9867		V
230	LA9818		V	280	LA9868		V
231	LA9819		V	281	LA9869		V
232	LA9820	*	V	282	LA9870	CS	V
233	LA9821		V	233	LA9871		V
234	LA9822		V	284	LA9872		V
235	LA9823	*r6	V	285	LA9873		V
236	LA9824		V	286	LA9874		V
237	LA9825		V	287	LA9875		V
238	LA9826		V	288	LA9876		V
239	LA9827		V	289	LA9877		V
240	LA9828	*r5ME(r)CS	V	290	LA9878		V
241	LA9829	*	V	291	LA9879		V
242	LA9830		V	292	LA9880		V
243	LA9831		V	293	LA9881		V
244	LA9832	ES	V	294	LA9882		V
245	LA9833		V	295	LA9883		V
246	LA9834		V	296	LA9884		V
247	LA9835		V	297	LA9885		V
248	LA9836	ME(r)	V	298	LA9886		V
249	LA9837		V	299	LA9887		V
250	LA9838		V	300	LA9888		V

301	LA9889		V	351	LA9939		A
302	LA9890	*r5	V	352	LA9940		J
303	LA9891	*r9	V	353	LA9941	*	J
304	LA9892		V	354	LA9942	*	J
305	LA9893	*	F	355	LA9943	d-ss	J
306	LA9894	*	F	356	LA9944	*	P
307	LA9895		F	357	LA9945		J
308	LA9896		F	358	LA9946	d-ss	J
309	LA9897		F	359	LA9947		J
310	LA9898		F	360	LA9948		X
311	LA9899	*	F	361	LA9949		X
312	LA9900		F	362	LA9950		X
313	LA9901	*	F	363	LA9951		X
314	LA9902		F	364	LA9952	ke	H
315	LA9903	*r5	F	365	LA9953		X
316	LA9904		F	366	LA9954		X
317	LA9905	*	H	367	LA9955		H
318	LA9906		F	368	LA9956		H
319	LA9907		F	369	LA9957		X
320	LA9908		F	370	LA9958		X
321	LA9909		F	371	LA9959		H
322	LA9910		F	372	LA9960		H
323	LA9911		F	373	LA9961	*	H
324	LA9912	ES	F	374	LA9962		H
325	LA9913		W	375	LA9963		X
326	LA9914		H	376	LA9964		H
327	LA9915	*	H	377	LA9965	*	H
328	LA9916	*r6 ME(r)	H	378	LA9966		H
329	LA9917	*r5	H	379	LA9967		X
330	LA9918	*	H	380	LA9968		H
331	LA9919	*r5 ME(r)	H	381	LA9969		H
332	LA9920	*	H	382	LA9970		H
333	LA9921	*r5	X	383	LA9971	*ke-L/196	H
334	LA9922		F	384	LA9972		X
335	LA9923		X	385	LA9973	*	H
336	LA9924		X	386	LA9974		H
337	LA9925	*r5	C	387	LA9975		H
338	LA9926		X	338	LA9976	*	H
339	LA9927		X	389	LN5999	L*	H
340	LA9928	*r5	X	390	LA9978	*r9	H
341	LA9929		C	391	LA9979	*	H
342	LA9930		J	392	LA9980	*r9	H
343	LA9931		J	393	LA9981	*	H
344	LA9932		X	394	LA9982		H
345	LA9933	*ke	X	395	LA9983		H
346	LA9934		X	396	LA9984		H
347	LA9935	*	H	397	LA9985		H
348	LA9936	*r6	J	398	LA9986		H
349	LA9937		J	399	LA9977		H
350	LA9938	*	J	400	LA9988	*	H

401	LA9989	*r5	H	451	LE9150			N
402	LA9990	*	H	452	LE9181			N
403	LA9991		H	453	LE9140	L-d		
404	LA9992	*	H	454	LE9167	*		C
405	LA9993		H	455	LE9033			D
406	LA9994	*r9	H	456	AN 660	*ke-		K
407	LE9065		C	457	AN 647			K
408	LA9996		P	458	LC4141			P
409	LA9997		K	459	LE9022			K
410	LA9998	*	K	460	LE9034	ES		P
411	LA9999		K	461	LN4573			P
412	LE9001	*	H	462	LE9032			P
413	LE9002	*r5	C	463	LE9015			D
414	LE9003		B	464	AN614			K
415	LE9004		B	465	LN7101			P
416	LE9005	*L/1 82	H	466	LN4576			P
417	LE9006		H	467	LE9018			P
418	LE9007		K	468	LN4568			P
419	LE9008		K	469	LN7102			P
420	LE9009		B	470	LN 286			N
421	LE9010		K	471	LE9019			D
422	LE9011	*re	H	472	LE9023	ME(r)		P
423	LE9012		B	473	LE9024			P
424	LE9013		B	474	LN4566			P
425	LE9014		H	475	LE9025			P
426	AN714		K	476	LE9026			D
427	LE9016		H	477	LE9027			P
428	LE9017		D	478	LE9029			P
429	AN664		K	479	LE9031			P
430	AN616		K	480	LE9035	ME(r)		P
431	LE9020		H	481	LE9036			P
432	LA9987		B	482	LC4143			P
433	LE9114	ME(*r)	N	483	LC5013			C
434	LE9111		B	484	A9107	*re ME (r)		U
435	LE9129		C	485	A9109-	*re		U
436	LE9136	L-d	J	486	LC5012			C
437	LE9137	L-ss-dES	P	487	A9154			U
438	LE9159	ME(r)	A	488	LC4138			N
439	LE9028		H	489	LN 288			P
440	LE9128		A	490	LE9039			P
441	LE9030			491	LE9044			P
442	LE9124	d-sx-st		492	LE9040			P
443	LE9127	d.ss	J	493	LE9038			N
444	LE9021		H	494	LN 287	*		N
445	LE9154	*L/192	C	495	LN 294	*r5		P
446	LE9151	*	B	496	LE9037			P
447	LE9175		A	497	LC3767			N
448	LE9170	* ke	P	498	LN 289			P
449	LE9156	* re	B	499	LN4584			P
450	LA9995		C	500	LE9041			P

501	LE9045		J	551	LE9067		J
502	LN4585		P	552	LE9072		P
503	LE9053	CS	P	553	LC8680	*	B
504	LE9048		K	554	LC4171		P
505	LE9050		J	555	LE9098		C
506	LE9049		K	556	LE9099		C
507	LE9057		K	557	LE9096	*	C
508	LE9906			558	LE9103	*	J
509	LE9054		K	559	LE9108		P
510	LE9043		J	560	LE9074		J
511	LE9063		J	561	LE9102		C
512	LE9042		J	562	LE9101	*	C
513	LE9064		J	563	LC4166		B
514	LE9047	ME(r)	J	564	LE9100		
515	LE9051		J	565	LE9104		P
516	LC4164		P	566	LE9122		P
517	LE9055		J	567	LC4168		P
518	LE9081		P	568	LE9077	ME(r)E	J
519	LE9046		P	569	LE9080		J
520	LE9056		J	570	LE9078	ME(r)	J
521	LE9061		K	571	LE9079		J
522	LE9066		J	572	LE9090		J
523	LE9060		K	573	LE9094		P
524	LE9092	ME(r)	J	574	LE9084		A
525	LE9089		J	575	LE9113		A
526	LC2200	AE	P	576	LC4172		P
527	LE9082		P	577	LE9088		T
528	LE9083		P	578	LE9112	*	B
529	LE9087	ME(r)	J	579	LE9158	*L/180	C
530	LE9085	ME(r)	J	580	LN 206	*	P
531	LE9086	*	J	581	LC4163		P
532	LE9091		J	582	LE9105		K
533	LE9093		C	583	LE9115		K
534	LE9062		K	584	LN4513	*re	B
535	LN7103		P	585	LE9117		B
536	LC3780		C	586	LE9118		
537	LN7105	ke	P	587	LE9110		P
538	LE9097	CS	J	588	LE9107	*	C
539	LE9058		K	589	LE9106		C
540	LE9073		K	590	LE9109	*	J
541	LE9059		K	591	LC8683		B
542	LE9052		K	592	LE9119		
543	LE9075		K	593	LN 219		P
544	LE9068		K	594	LE9153		N
545	LE9076		P	595	LE9121	*ke	J
546	LN4583	*	P	596	LC8667	*	B
547	LE9071		K	597	LE9116	*re	J
548	LE9069		J	598	LE9120	*	J
549	LE9070		J	599	LE9162		N
550	LE9095		C	600	LE9155	*ke	B

601	LE9179		S		651	LE9187		C
602	LN218		P		652	LE9292	ME(r)	R
603	LN207		P		653	LN4521	*	S
604	LE9123		A		654	LN4525	*ke	T
605	LC2323	*	T		655	LE9244		D
606	LE9126	*	J		666	A9142		U
607	LE9130	*	C		657	LE9169	*L/173	S
608	LE9125	*r5ME(r)	J		658	LE9235	*ke	R
609	LN7120		P		659	LE9242	*	P
610	A9145	*re	U		660	LE9236	*	P
611	LN223		N		661	LE9205	ME(r)	G
612	A9119		U		662	LC5052	*	S
613	LE9213		T		663	LE9186		F
614	LE9157	*	F		664	LE9161	*r6 CS	D
615	LE9226	*	T		665	LE9163		G
616	LE9168	*	D		666	LN319		G
617	A9113		U		667	LE9166		N
618	A9133		U		668	LE9198	*re	D
619	LE9234	*	A		669	LE9183	ES	D
620	LE9173	*	B		670	LE9192		D
621	LE9178		S		671	LE9180		S
622	LE9229	d-st	T		672	LE9184	*	S
623	LE9216	ME(t)	B		673	LE9217		D
624	LE9114		S		674	LE9195		D
625	LE9182	*	B		675	LE9197		D
626	LN307		P		676	LE9214		D
627	A9132		U		677	LE9196		D
628	A9177		U		678	LE9203		T
629	LN291		T		679	A9166	*	U
630	LE9177		D		680	LE9215		G
631	LE9193		D		681	LE9208	ME(r)	F
632	LN242	d-sx	N		682	LE9176		G
633	LE9200		T		683	LE9194		F
634	LE9152	*r5	J		684	LC5018	*ke	D
635	LE9165	*r5	C		685	LE9185	.	P
636	LN4528		A		686	A9168	. r9	U
637	LN4518		T		687	LE9172		P
638	LN7119		P		688	LN331		P
639	LE9231	*	T		689	LE9211		D
640	LE9164		C		690	LE9171	*	B
641	LE9202		T		691	LE9199	8ke	B
642	LE9207		D		692	LE9221		D
643	LE9241	*	B		693	LE9206		D
644	LE9160	*	C		694	LE9219	*re	R
645	LN293		P		695	LE9191		R
646	A9173		U		696	LE9209	*	B
647	A9144		U		697	LE9210		R
648	LN311		P		698	LE9190		R
649	LE9189		D		699	LE9204		R
650	LE9201		D		700	LE9270		C

701	LE9212		T	751	LE9225	ME(r)	R
702	LE9218	*re-L/9	T	752	LE9401	L*	
703	LE9403	L/10		753	LE9145	L-ke	
704	LE9222	*	T	754	LE9889		J
705	LE9220	*	T	755	LE9258		B
706	LE9230	*	T	756	LE9253	*	T
707	LE9224	ke	A	757	LE9259		P
708	LE9248	*	B	758	LE9276		P
709	LE9240	*re	B	759	LE9232		B
710	LE9245	*r5 ME(r)	S	760	LE9263		P
711	LE9247	*	S	761	LE9252	*	D
712	LE9238		N	762	LE9255		A
713	LE9239	*	T	763	LE9266	*	P
714	LE9243	*	T	764	LE9254	*L/169	F
715	LE9188	*r9	R	765	LE9256	*	C
716	LE9227	*	T	766	LE9262	*	C
717	LE9141	L-d		767	LE9264	*ke	C
718	LE9251	*r9	S	768	LE9269		B
719	LE9249		N	769	LE9265	*	S
720	LE9143	L-d ME (r)		770	LE9274		P
721	LE9246	*ke	S	771	LE9275	*	F
722	LE9250	*	D	772	LE9281		P
723	LE9146	L-d		773	LE9282		P
724	LE9404	L		774	LE9268	*L/154	B
725	LE9148	L-ss-d ES		775	LE9271	*	P
726	LE9149	L-d ME (r)		776	LE9273	*r6	S
727	LE9147	L-ss.d	F	777	LE9272	*L/163	D
728	LE9903		P	778	LE9267	*r5	S
729	LE9144	L-d ME (r)		779	LE9278	*	S
730	LE9405	L		780	LE9280	*	D
731	LE9402	L-d ME(r)		781	LE9288		N
732	LE9913		W	782	LE9293	*ke	D
733	LE9914		W	783	LE9277	*	D
734	LE9915		H	784	LE9294	*	D
735	LE9888		S	785	LE9291	*ke	N
736	LE9228	*re	C	786	LE9279	*r5	D
737	LE9261	ME(r)	N	787	LE9295	*r5	G
738	LE9912	*	G	788	LE9298	*	G
739	LE9142	*L-d ME(r)		789	LE9285	*	D
740	LE9290		P	790	LE9286	*ke-sx	P
741	LE9233	*ME(r)	B	791	LE9284	*re	G
742	LE9223		B	792	LE9287	*	p
743	LE9887		M	793	LE9332	*	S
744	LE9314	ke	S	794	LE9438	*r5	G
745	LE9283		F	795	LE9297	*r6 ME(r)	P
746	LE9890		Q	796	LE9304	*ke	A
747	LE9257		B	797	LE9437	*	A
748	LE9260		B	798	LE9457		P
749	LE9891		V	799	LE9289		P
750	LE9237	ME(r)	B	800	LE9296		N

801	LE9301	*re	P	851	LE9345		D
802	LE9338	*	B	852	LE9342		R
803	LE9303	*	S	853	LE9346	*re	C
804	LE9347	*ME(r)	N	854	LE9341	*	P
805	LE9339	*	A	855	LE9326		C
806	LE9299	*	P	856	LE9344	*	P
807	LE9355		B	857	LE9475		P
808	LE9306		F	858	LE9348	*	P
809	LE9365	*	G	859	LE9328		F
810	LE9307	*	S	860	LE9382		D
811	LE9325		S	861	LE9381	*	A
812	LE9305	*	S	862	LE9466		
813	LE9302	*ke	P	863	LE9333	*	N
814	LE9335		B	864	LE9461		p
815	LE9321		B	865	LF9366	ME(r)	S
816	LE9319	*	A	866	LE9398		A
817	LE9329		T	867	LE9369		R
818	LE9308		R	868	LE9386	ME(r)	B
819	LE9323	*	G	869	LE9464	*	A
820	LE9310		B	870	LF9336		T
821	LE9320	*r9	C	871	LE9337	*	F
822	LE9300	ME (r)	S	872	LE9343	*	N
823	LE9360	*	G	873	LE9353		S
824	LE9367		S	874	LE9362		D
825	LE9357	*	G	875	LE9340	*	S
826	LE9309	*r5	B	876	LE9350		D
827	LE9322	*re	D	877	LE9370		S
828	LE9315	*	D	878	LE9361		D
829	LE9354	*	A	879	LE9427		R
830	LE9359	*	A	880	LE9358	*	F
831	LE9324		R	881	LE9351		D
832	LE9313	*	T	882	LE9364	*	F
833	LE9439	*r5	C	883	LE9378		P
834	LE9311		N	884	LE9363		D
835	LE9316	*	T	885	LE9380	*r5	S
836	LE9312	*	T	886	LE9368	*	N
837	LE9387	*r5	C	887	LE9383	*	A
838	LE9318		N	888	LE9372		D
839	LE9440		C	889	LE9356		S
840	LE9444	*e	F	890	LE9371		D
841	LE9388		C	891	LE9373		D
842	LE9317	*	T	892	LE9377		D
843	LE9441	*r9	G	893	LE9375		B
844	LE9331		D	894	LE9376	*	B
845	LE9330		C	895	LE9379	*	S
846	LE9327	*	G	896	LE9385	*	A
847	LE9458		P	897	LE9384	*	G
848	LE9334		D	898	LE9374		R
849	LE9352		C	899	LE9389	ME(r)	B
850	LE9349	*ke	F	900	LE9397	*	G

901	LE9393		D	951	LE9474		AB
902	LE9390		F	952	LE9436		F
903	LE9394		D	953	LE9479		F
904	LE9392		D	954	LE9500		T
905	LE9391		C	955	LE9786	*L/1 86	G
906	LE9395		C	956	LE9470		R
907	LE9426		P	957	LE9489		D
908	LE9399		B	958	LE9477		B
909	LE9400		J	959	LE9752		T
910	LE9421		J	960	LE9496	CS	R
911	LE9480	NO	P	961	LE9472	*L/1 89	G
912	LE9396	*re	J	962	LE9486		B
913	LE9425		J	963	LE9491		T
914	LE9422		D	964	LE9463	*	F
915	LE9423		D	965	LE9494		AB
916	LE9424		B	966	LE9499		T
917	LE9429		B	967	LE9488	CS	P
918	LE9428		B	968	LE9498		AB
919	LE9432	*	G	969	LE9469		P
920	LE9431	*r5 CS	G	970	LE9478		P
921	LE9430		AB	971	LE9483		P
922	LE9443	CS AE	P	972	LE9484	CS	P
923	LE9433		C	973	LE9493		T
924	LE9435		C	974	LE9497		N
925	LE9442	d-sx	R	975	LE9492		T
926	LE9446		S	976	LE9755		J
927	LE9447		B	977	LE9481		B
928	LE9448		R	978	LE9468		P
929	LE9467		A	979	LE9751		P
930	LE9434		D	980	LE9764	CS	AB
931	LE9465		D	981	LE9753		T
932	LE9445		B	982	LE9760		P
933	LE9451		B	983	LE9462		P
934	LE9450		B	984	LE9764		P
935	LE9456		P	985	LE9759		P
936	LE9449		A	986	LE9762		P
937	LE9459		B	987	LE9758		P
938	LE9452		P	988	LE9763		P
939	LE9453		P	989	LE9766	ES	T
940	LE9783		A	990	LE9772		AB
941	LE9460		F	991	LE9756	ME(r)	J
942	LE9490		T	992	LE9757		J
943	LE9487	CS	A	993	LE9765		P
944	LE9471		AB	994	LE9844	ME(r)	AB
945	LE9454		P	995	LE9767	*	AB
946	LE9455		P	996	LE9774	*ke	AB
947	LE9485	d-ss-d re	C	997	LE9771		P
948	LE9476		P	998	LE9761		AB
949	LE9482		D	999	LE9768		T
950	LE9473		AB	1000	LE9999	sb*	

1001	LE9770	*	G	1051	LE9814		A
1002	LE9778	*	G	1052	LE9805	*r6	G
1003	LE9773		AB	1053	LE9813		A
1004	LE9777	*	G	1054	LE9812		B
1005	LE9769	*r9	G	1055	LE9822	*r6 ME (r)	C
1006	LE9779		A	1056	LE9819		N
1007	LE9776		A	1057	LE9818		B
1008	LE9798		D	1058	LE9823	d-st	T
1009	LE9782	ke	A	1059	LE9821		A
1010	LE9775	*ke	N	1060	LE9820	L/183	A
1011	LE9791		R	1061	LE9826		R
1012	LE9780		N	1062	LE9829		C
1013	LE9781		B	1063	LE9828		B
1014	LE9787		B	1064	LE9830	d-ch(C 4)	T
1015	LE9785	*	C	1065	LE9831		R
1016	LE9408	L-d ME(r)		1066	LE9824		T
1017	LE9411	L/12		1067	LE9835		T
1018	LE9409	L/11		1068	LE9832		D
1019	LE9789		D	1069	LE9836		B
1020	LE9793		F	1070	LE9833		N
1021	LN336	L		1071	LE9839		D
1022	LE9790		D	1072	LE9834		D
1023	LE9495		AB	1073	LE9843	ke	R
1024	LE9788		D	1074	LE9852		AB
1025	LE9784		A	1075	LE9840		R
1026	LE9817		R	1076	LE9842		D
1027	LE9412	L-d		1077	LE9841		T
1028	LE9809		F	1078	LE9838		D
1029	LE9792		D	1079	LE9846	*r5	C
1030	LE9810		R	1080	LE9837		D
1031	LE9811		A	1081	LE9847		D
1032	LE9796		AB	1082	LE9848		D
1033	LE9801		A	1083	LE9860		B
1034	LE9794	*re	F	1084	LE9849		D
1035	LE9802		B	1085	LE9858		D
1036	LE9800		D	1086	LE9845		AB
1037	LE9850		R	1087	LE9856		D
1038	LE9807	*	C	1088	LE9857		N
1039	LE9803		D	1089	LE9855		T
1040	LE9827		F	1090	LE9853		B
1041	LE9806		D	1091	LE9859		B
1042	LE9808		N	1092	LE9861		AB
1043	LE9815		D	1093	LE9873		AB
1044	LE9795		B	1094	LE9867		T
1045	LE9797		B	1095	LE9871	*re	AB
1046	LE9851		N	1096	LE9854	*	T
1047	LE9816		D	1097	LE9863		J
1048	LE9799		F	1098	LE9869		J
1049	LE9804		N	1099	LE9868		J
1050	LE9825		F	1100	LE9862		B

1101	LE9864	*	AB	1151	LE9930		J
1102	LE9865	*r5	AB	1152	LE9932		J
1103	LE9870	*ke	AB	1153	LE9959		W
1104	LE9872		F	1154	LE9907		P
1105	LE9866	*	AB	1155	LE9904		E
1106	LE9879	*	AB	1156	LE9948		W
1107	LE9880	*r9	AB	1157	LE9938		W
1108	LE9876	CS	AB	1158	LE9939		W
1109	LE9878		AB	1159	LE9947		W
1110	LE9881	AE	AB	1160	LE9905		F
1111	LE9893	AE	AB	1161	LE9942		J
1112	LE9885		S	1162	LE9957		W
1113	LE9875		AB	1163	LE9908		D
1114	LE9877		J	1164	LE9909	CS	D
1115	LE9923		AB	1165	LE9937		J
1116	LE9874		S	1166	LE9935		J
1117	LE9882		AB	1167	LE9943		J
1118	LE9884		AB	1168	LE9945		J
1119	LE9886		F	1169	LE9946		J
1120	LE9883		AB	1170	LE9936	ES	B
1121	LE9922		AB	1171	LE9944		B
1122	LE9916		AB	1172	LE9950		J
1123	LE9892		T	1173	LE9951		J
1124	LE9920		AB	1174	LE9949		J
1125	LE9894		AB	1175	LE9954		J
1126	LE9925	CS	AB	1176	LE9952		J
1127	LE9917		J	1177	LF8001		J
1128	LE9941		AB	1178	LE9955		J
1129	LE9902		J	1179	LE9962		J
1130	LE9897		AB	1180	LE9973		W
1131	LE9921		AB	1181	LE9953		J
1132	LE9940		AB	1182	LE9961		J
1133	LE9918		AB	1183	LE9956		J
1134	LE9895		AB	1184	LE9410	L-d	AB
1135	LE9924		AB	1185	LE9963	*L/168	J
1136	LE9896		AB	1186	LE9964	CS	J
1137	LE9901			1187	LE9958		W
1138	LE9926		AB	1188	LE9968		J
1139	LE9919		AB	1189	LE9972	ME(r)	W
1140	LE9927		J	1190	LE9978		B
1141	LE9928		J	1191	LE9960		J
1142	LE9899		AB	1192	LE9970		A
1143	LE9898		J	1193	LE9984		A
1144	LE9934		J	1194	LE9985		R
1145	LE9900		J	1195	LE9965		A
1146	LE9911	ES	A	1196	LE 9967		J
1147	LE9910	ES	D	1197	LE9966		A
1148	LE9981		J	1198	LE9969		J
1149	LE9929		J	1199	LE9971		J
1150	LE9933		J	1200	LE9974		J

1201	LE9976	d-L/23	N	1251	LF8031		N
1202	LE9975		C	1252	LF8032		N
1203	LE9998		F	1253	LF8033		X
1204	LE9993		G	1254	LE8034		AB
1205	LE9977		C	1255	LE8035		X
1206	LF9982		G	1266	LF8036		T
1207	LE9980		E	1257	LF8037	ES	T
1208	LE9989		G	1258	LF8038		D
1209	LE9979		C	1259	LF8039		F
1210	LE9981		G	1260	LF8040		T
1211	LE9988	*	G	1261	LF8041		D
1212	LE9983		G	1262	LF8042		B
1213	LE9991		E	1263	LF8043	d-ch(CI)	B
1214	LE9986	ES	B	1264	LF8044		S
1215	LE9987	ke	F	1265	LF8045		A
1216	LF8003	*	Q	1266	LF8046		P
1217	LF8002		G	1267	LF8047		P
1218	LE9990		B	1268	LF8048		P
1219	LF8004	*	J	1269	LF8049		S
1220	LE9997		B	1270	LF8050		K
1221	LE9992		B	1271	LF8051	CS	K
1222	LE9996		J	1272	LF8052	*	F
1223	LE9994		J	1273	LF8053		F
1224	LE9995		J	1274	LF8054	*	K
1225	LF8005		J	1275	LF8055		K
1226	LF8006		J	1276	LF8056		K
1227	LF8007		F	1277	LF8057		AB
1228	LF8008		J	1278	LF8058		AB
1229	LF8009	d-ss-st	F	1279	LF8059		K
1230	LF8010		J	1280	LF8060		K
1231	LF8011		J	1281	LF8061	*r5	K
1232	LF8012		J	1282	LF8062		AB
1233	LF8013		J	1283	LF8063		AB
1234	LF8014		J	1284	LF8064	*r5	K
1235	LF8015		AD	1285	LF8065		B
1236	LF8016		J	1286	LF8066		AB
1237	LF8017		G	1287	LF8067		AB
1238	LF8018		G	1288	LF8068		K
1239	LF8019		D	1289	LF8069	d-sx	K
1240	LF8020	*re	AD	1290	LF8070	*r5 ME (r)	K
1241	LF8021		G	1291	LF8071		AB
1242	LF8022		G	1292	LF8072		K
1243	LF8023		G	1293	LF8073		AB
1244	LF8024		F	1294	LF8074		H
1245	LF8025		G	1295	LF8075		AB
1246	LF8026		G	1296	LF8076	*	K
1247	LF9980	c- L-d		1297	LF8077	*	T
1248	LF8028	*	F	1298	LF8078	*r5	K
1249	LF8029		G	1299	LF8079		T
1250	LF8030		K	1300	LF8080	*	K

1301	LF8081	* r5-L/33	K	1351	LF8131		G
1302	LF8082	d-L	T	1352	LF8132		F
1303	LF8083		K	1353	LF8133		F
1304	LF8084	*	K	1354	LE9416	ch*	H
1305	LF8085	*	K	1355	LF8135		C
1306	LF8086		K	1356	LF8136		G
1307	LF8087	CS	T	1357	LE9415	ch*re	H
1308	LF8088		H	1358	LF8138		G
1309	LF8089	*r9	T	1359	LF8139		G
1310	LF3090	*	T	1360	LF8140		P
1311	LF8091		T	1361	LF8141		G
1312	LF8092		T	1362	LF8142		G
1313	LF8093	*	K	1363	LF8143		G
1314	LF8094		B	1364	LF8144		G
1315	LF8095	*re	K	1365	LF8145		G
1316	LF8096	*r5	K	1366	LF8146		G
1317	LF8097	d-ss-re	F	1367	LF8147	*r5 ME(r)	G
1318	LF8098	*ke	K	1368	LF8148		G
1319	LF8099	d-L	K	1369	LF8149		G
1320	LF8100	ke	K	1370	LF8150		G
1321	LF8101	*ke	AD	1371	LF8151		G
1322	LF8102		AD	1372	LF8152	*r9	G
1323	LF8103	*	AD	1373	LF8153	ke	G
1324	LF8104	*ke	K	1374	LN299	L-d	
1325	LF8105		AD	1375	LF8155	*r9	G
1326	LF8106	*	T	1376	LF8156		G
1327	LF8107	*r9	K	1377	LF8157	*	G
1328	LF8108		G	1378	LF8158		G
1329	LF8109		AD	1379	LF8159	*ke-L	G
1330	LF8110		AD	1380	LF8160	*re,	G
1331	LF8111		AD	1381	LF8161	*	G
1332	LF8112		S	1382	LF8224	L-dME(r)NO	
1333	LF8113		AD	1383	LF8163		G
1334	LF8114		AD	1384	LF8164	*r5 ME(r)	G
1335	LFB115		AF	1385	LF8165		G
1336	LF8116		AF	1386	LF8166		G
1337	LF8117		T	1387	LF8223	L-d	G
1338	LF8118		T	1388	LF8168		G
1339	LF8119		T	1389	LF8169		N
1340	LF8120		T	1390	LF8170		G
1341	LF8121		T	1391	LF8222	L-ss	AD
1342	LF8122	CS	G	1392	LF8167		G
1343	LF8123		G	1393	LF8226	L*	D
1344	LF8124		T	1394	LF8225	sb-st	
1345	LF8125		H	1395	LF8175		G
1346	LF8126		G	1396	LF8181		G
1347	LF8127		G	1397	LF8228	L/44	
1348	LF8128		G	1398	LF8229	L-d	A
1349	LF8129		G	1399	LF8221	L-d	B
1350	LF8130	*r5 ME(r)	T	1400	LF8227	L-d	K

1401	LF8173	*ke ES	H		1451	LF8213		D
1402	LF8171		H		1452	LF8211		D
1403	LF8183		G		1453	LF8214		D
1404	LF8230	L-ss-d-re	F		1454	LF8235		N
1405	LF8172	*	H		1455	LF8217		D
1406	LF8154	*	G		1456	LF8215	*L/1 79	N
1407	LF8162		G		1457	LF8216	CS	N
1408	LF8182	*	G		1458	LF8232		N
1409	LF8027	ke	H		1459	LF8233		W
1410	LF8185		H		1460	LF8234	*	
1411	LF8184		T		1461	LF8246		
1412	LF8191	*r9	H		1462	LF8236	*ke	
1413	LF8177	*ke	H		1463	LF8244		W
1414	LF8178		N		1464	LF8238		S
1415	LF8134		H		1465	LF8237		A
1416	LF8174	*	H		1466	LF8240		P
1417	LF8197	*ke	H		1467	LF8247		W
1418	LF8137		H		1468	LF8245		AD
1419	LF8199		H		1469	LF8239		A
1420	LF8180	ES	H		1470	LF8248	*	N
1421	LF8176	*	H		1471	LF8241		P
1422	LF8187	*ke	H		1472	LF8251	L/157	N
1423	LF8186	*	H		1473	LF8249		N
1424	LF8188	*r6 CS	AD		1474	LF8242		P
1425	LF8300	sb	J		1475	LF8243		N
1426	LF8190	*	AD		1476	LF8250		N
1427	LF8189		T		1477	LF8252	ME(r)	N
1423	LF8200		N		1478	LF8258		N
1429	LF8201		N		1479	LF8259	*	N
1430	LF8202		N		1480	LF8260	*	AD
1431	LF8192		N		1481	LF8276		N
1432	LF8193		N		1482	LF8256		N
1433	LF8194		N		1483	LF8257		T
1434	LF8203	ke	W		1484	LF8254		T
1435	LF8179		N		1485	LF8255		T
1436	LF8196	L*	AD		1486	LF8253		N
1437	LF8219		N		1487	LF8261		N
1438	LF8208		N		1488	LF8265		N
1439	LF8206		T		1489	LF8275		N
1440	LF8198	ES	H		1490	LF8266	*	AD
1441	LF8195	*	AD		1491	LF8277	*r5	AD
1442	LF8231		N		1492	LF8278		N
1443	LF8205		AD		1493	LF8262		N
1444	LF8209		N		1494	LF8279		N
1445	LF8220		N		1495	LF8263		N
1446	LF8207	*r6	AD		1496	LF8264		D
1447	LF8283		N		1497	LF8269	CS	G
1448	LF8204	*	H		1498	LF8268		T
1449	LF8210	*	AD		1499	LF8273	sb	
1450	LF8212		AD		1500	LF8267		AD

1501	LF8280	*	AD	1551	LF8321			E
1502	LF8281	*ke ES	AD	1552	LF8323			N
1503	LF8270		AD	1553	LF8330		*	N
1504	LF8271	ke	E	1554	LF8324			T
1505	LF8274		N	1555	LF8331			F
1506	LF8295		Q	1556	LF8333			AD
1507	LF8282		AD	1557	LF8329			AD
1508	LF8283		AD	1558	LF8332			B
1509	LF8272	ke	E	1559	LF8343			AD
1510	LF8284		T	1560	LF8340			E
1511	LF8289	*	Q	1561	LF8337			AD
1512	LF8287		E	1562	LF8335			AD
1513	LF8291		AD	1563	LF8338			AD
1514	LF8288	d-L	E	1564	LF8334			AD
1515	LF8301		N	1565	LF8344			AD
1516	LF8290		T	1566	LF8336			AD
1517	LF8286		N	1567	LF8341			B
1518	LF8285		T	1568	LF8345			AD
1519	LF8292	*	AD	1669	LF8346			AD
1520	LF8296		N	1570	LE8339			AD
1521	LF8298		N	1571	LE8349			T
1522	LF8311		K	1572	LF8342			T
1523	LF8299	d-L	N	1573	LF8362			AD
1524	LF8294		N	1574	LF8354		d-ss-st	AD
1525	LF8297		N	1575	LF8351			AD
1526	LF8293		Q	1576	LF8350			T
1527	LF8304,	d-L/50	B	1577	LF8353			AD
1528	LF8305		T	1578	LE8352			AD
1529	LE8306		N	1579	LF8347			T
1530	LF8303		B	1580	LF8348			AD
1531	LF8302		B	1581	LF8355			AD
1532	LF8312		K	1582	LF8361			AD
1533	LF8646	L		1583	LF8356			AD
1534	LF8309		B	1584	LF8358			AD
1535	LF8308		B	1585	LF8357			AD
1536	LF8307		AD	1586	LF8363			AD
1637	LF8310		B	1587	LF8364		ES	AD
1538	LF8313	*	Q	1588	LF8365		d-ch (C2)	AD
1539	LF8314		AD	1589	LF8366			AD
1540	LF8320	ME(r)	N	1590	LF8367			AD
1541	LF8325	*	F	1591	LF8368			AD
1542	LF8326	*	F	1592	LF8360			AD
1543	LF8322	*	B	1593	LF8371			AD
1544	LF8327		Q	1594	LF8359			AD
1545	LF8316		T	1595	LF8372			AD
1546	LF8317		T	1596	LF8370			T
1547	LF8315		AD	1597	LF8369			AD
1548	LF8328		F	1598	LF8381			AD
1549	LF8318		AD	1599	LF8382			T
1550	LF8319		AD	1600	LF8373			AD

1601	LF8383		AD	1651	LF8428			AF
1602	LF8376		T	1662	LF8427			AF
1603	LF8378	ES	T	1653	LF8426			AF
1604	LF8379		T	1654	LF8420			AF
1605	LF8374		T	1855	LF8429			AD
1606	LF8377		T	1656	LF8441	ME(r)		B
1607	LF8380		T	1657	LF8442			AD
1608	LF8384		AD	1668	LF8443			AD
1609	LF8375		T	1659	LF8430	d-st		AD
1610	LF8393		AD	1660	LF8431	*		AD
1611	LF8395		AD	1661	LF8439			AF
1612	LF8385		AD	1662	LF8436			AF
1613	LF8386		AD	1663	LF8438			AF
1614	LF8394	d-sx	AD	1664	LF8434			AF
1615	LF8387		AD	1665	LF8447	*re		AD
1616	LF8396		T	1666	LF8437			AF
1617	LF8389		AD	1667	LF8444			R
1618	LF8392		A.D	1668	LF8445			P
1619	LF8388		AD	1669	LF8433			AF
1620	LF8402	ME(r)	AD	1670	LF8446			P
1621	LF8390		AD	1671	LF8435			AF
1622	LF8391		AD	1672	LF8432			T
1623	LF8397		T	1673	LF8454			AF
1624	LF8403		T	1674	LF8451			P
1625	LF8401		T	1675	LF8448			P
1626	LF8404		T	1676	LF8455			AF
1627	LF8398		T	1677	LF8449			P
1628	LF8405		T	1678	LF8458			AF
1629	LF8399		AD	1679	LF8456			P
1630	LF8406	ES	AD	1680	LF8461			AF
1631	LF8407		AD	1681	LF8450			AF
1632	LF8409	ke	AD	1682	LF8460			AF
1633	LF8408		AD	1683	LF8457			AF
1634	LF8400		T	1684	LF8459			T
1636	LF8410		AD	1685	LF8462			AF
1636	LF8413		T	1686	LF8467			AF
1637	LF8412	*re	AD	1687	LF8452			AF
1938	LF8414		AD	1688	LF8453			AF
1639	LF8411		AD	1689	LF8476			AF
1640	LF8415		T	1690	LF8464			AF
1641	LF8417		AD	1691	LF8469			AF
1642	LF8422		AE	1602	LF8475			AF
1643	LF8423		AD	1693	LF8463	ES		AF
1644	LF8416		S	1694	LF8472			AF
1645	LF8424		S	1695	LF8473	CS		AF
1646	LF8421		T	1696	LF8468	ME(r)		AF
1647	LF8425		AF	1697	LF8470			AF
1648	LF8418		AD	1698	LF8474	*ke		A
1649	LF8419		AD	1699	LF8465			AF
1650	LF8440	d-ss-ke	AD	1700	LF8478	ES		AF

1701	LF8471		AF	1751	LF8522	*	R
1702	LF8479		AF	1752	LF8516	*	R
1703	LF8477		AF	1753	LF8525		AF
1704	LF8466		AF	1754	LF8535		AF
1705	LF8485		AF	1755	LF8518	ke	S
1706	LF8482		A	1756	LF8524		AF
1707	LF8480		AF	1757	LF8523		S
1708	LF8481		AF	1758	LF8591	L*	S
1709	LF8484		AF	1759	LF8534	*	AF
1710	LF8486		AF	1760	LF8526		AF
1711	LF8487	ME(r)	AF	1761	LF8521		AF
1712	LF8483		AF	1762	LF8520	*	C
1713	LF8488		AF	1763	LF8545		AF
1714	LF8494		AF	1764	LF8531		AF
1715	LF8490		AF	1765	LF8527	* ke	AF
1716	LF8489		AF	1766	LF8542		AF
1717	LF8497		B	1767	LF8540		T
1718	LF8491		AF	1768	LF8533		AF
1719	LF8492		AF	1769	LF8541	*	AF
1720	LF8493	*	R	1770	LF8547		AF
1721	LE9419	L-ss-st		1771	LF8543		AF
1722	LE9417	L-d-sx NO		1772	LF8549	*ke	AF
1723	LF8495		B	1773	LF8544		AF
1724	LF8496		D	1774	LF8552		AF
1725	LF8499		D	1775	LF8539		R
1726	LF8498		D	1776	LF8555		R
1727	LF8500		F	1777	LF8538	*rx	R
1728	LE9420	L-ss-re	AF	1778	LF8537	*	R
1729	LE9418	L-d-ME(r)		1779	LF8551		T
1730	LF8501		F	1780	LF8536	*ke	AF
1731	LF8505		R	1781	LF8550		AF
1732	LF8502	ES	E	1782	LF8568	*re	R
1733	LF8514		E	1783	LF8548	ME(r	AF
1734	LF8504		E	1784	LF8546	*	AF
1735	LF8512		S	1785	LF8553		B
1736	LF8513	L	S	1786	LF8557		R
1737	LF8507		S	1787	LF8558		S
1738	LF8506		AF	1788	LF8556		S
1739	LF8515		AF	1789	LF8560		S
1740	LF8509		A	1790	LF8561	*	R
1741	LF8503		A	1791	LF8554		D
1742	LF8511	d-sx	D	1792	LF8566	*	R
1743	LF8508		D	1793	LF8563		S
1744	LF8532		T	1794	LF8564		AF
1745	LF8528		AF	1795	LF8565	ES	S
1746	LF8529		T	1796	LF8567	*r5	G
1747	LF8517	ME(r)	D	1797	LF8559		S
1748	LF8519	CS	F	1793	LF8570		B
1749	LF8530		AF	1799	LF8562		D
1750	LF8510	ES	F	1800	LF8571		C

1801	LF8572		T	1851	LF8622		G
1802	LF8569		A	1852	LF8640		G
1803	LF8573		T	1853	LF8617		G
1804	LF8585		G	1854	LF8614		T
1805	LF8574	*	D	1855	LF8623		D
1806	LF8583		G	1856	LF8624		F
1807	LF8582		G	1857	LF8625	*ke	B
1808	LF8584		AC	1858	LF8639	sb	V
1809	LF8581	d-L	A	1859	LF8626		A
1810	LF8589		A	1860	LF8627		E
1811	LF8588	ME(r)	A	1861	LF8630		H
1812	LF8587		C	1862	LF8616		B
1813	LF8586		C	1863	LF8629		B
1814	LF8575	ME(r)	D	1864	LF8634		B
1815	LF8576		F	1865	LF8632		B
1816	LF8577		E	1866	LF8648	*r5	H
1817	LF8578	(ss-d)	C	1867	LF8633	*	B
1818	LF8579	ES		1868	LF8651	*	B
1819	LF8580		B	1869	LF8631		G
1820	LF8595		C	1870	LF8638		F
1821	LF8590	*	G	1871	LF8656	ss-d	C
1822	LF8597		T	1872	LF8628		E
1823	LF8596	AE	F	1873	LF8670	sb	B
1824	LF8598		T	1874	LF8637		E
1825	LF8594		E	1875	LF8641		F
1826	LF8601		G	1876	LF8636		D
1827	LF8593		C	1877	LF8657	*ke	C
1828	LF8609	ss-d	C	1878	LF8635		C
1829	LF8600	*ke	E	1879	LF8658	ss-d	C
1830	LF8610	ME(r)	D	1880	LF8653		D
1831	LF8644	L-d		1881	LF8659	ss-d	C
1832	LF8643	L-d ME(r)		1882	LF8650		D
1833	LF8645	L-ss-d		1883	LF8642		D
1834	LF8592		R	1884	LF8649		D
1835	LF8611		E	1885	LF8666		D
1836	LF8603	ss-d-re	G	1886	LF8660		S
1837	LF8599	*L/178	B	1887	LF8652	*	S
1838	LF8602		G	1888	LF8663		D
1839	LF8618		B	1889	LF9316	MS	AC
1840	LF8607		D	1890	LF8654	AE	F
1841	LF8619		D	1891	LF8655		E
1842	LF8605	d-ss	G	1892	LF8662		A
1843	LF8821		D	1893	LF8661		H
1844	LF8604		G	1894	LF8665		F
1845	LF8608		D	1895	LF8664	*re	F
1846	LF8606		D	1896	LF8669		E
1847	LF8620		G	1897	LF8679		F
1848	LF8612		D	1898	LF8668		T
1849	LF8613		T	1899	LF8680		E
1850	LF8615		T	1900	LF8674		E

Year	Code	Mid	Right	Year	Code	Mid	Right
1901	LF8675		E	1951	LF9280	AS	J
1902	LF8667		T	1952	LF9279	AS	J
1903	LF8671		E	1953	LF9283	AS*	J
1904	LF8672		E	1954	LF9296	AS*	J
1905	LF8673	*	E	1955	LF9286	AS*	J
1906	LF9255	AS	J	1956	LF9298	AS*	J
1907	LF8676		E	1957	LF9289	AS	A
1908	LF9256	AS	J	1958	LF9290	AS	A
1909	LF9259	AS	J	1959	LF9313	MS	AC
1910	LF9258	AS CS AE	J	1960	LF9293	AS*	J
1911	LF9257	AS	AD	1961	LF9291	AS*r9	S
1912	LF8681		F	1962	LF8692	*	T
1913	LF8683		AC	1963	LF9292	AS	A
1914	LF8682		E	1964	LF9288	AS	A
1915	LF9263	AS	AD	1965	LF9295	AS	A
1916	LF8684		E	1966	LF8691		E
1917	LF9260	AS	J	1967	LF9299	AS	A
1918	LF8686	ss-d	C	1968	LF9294	AS	A
1919	LF8687	ss-d	C	1969	LF9297	AS	A
1920	LF9272	AS	J	1970	LF9318	MS	AC
1921	LF9271	AS	J	1971	LF9310	MS	AC
1922	LF9261	AS	AD	1972	LF9320	MS	AC
1923	LF9264	AS CS	J	1973	LF9323	MS	AC
1924	LF8685	ME(r)	AF	1974	LF9314	MS	AC
1925	LF8688	ss-d*re	C	1975	LF9317	MS AE	AC
1926	LF9262	AS	J	1976	LF9309	AS	S
1927	LF8689	ss-d*	C	1977	LF9319	MS	AC
1928	LF9273	AS	J	1978	LF9300	AS	S
1929	LF9270	AS	J	1979	LF9301	AS	S
1930	LF9287	AS	AD	1980	LF9321	MS	AC
1931	LF9278	AS	AD	1981	LF9322	MS	AC
1932	LF9265	AS	AD	1982	LF9303	AS	S
1933	LF8678		E	1983	LF9308	AS	S
1934	LF9275	AS	A	1984	LF9325	MS	AC
1935	LF9311	MS	AC	1985	LF9302	AS	S
1936	LF9277	AS	AD	1986	LF9324	MS	AC
1937	LF9276	AS	AD	1987	LF9326	MS	AC
1938	LF9269	AS*r6	J	1988	LF9333	MS	AC
1939	LF9268	AS	AD	1989	LF8693	*	
1940	LF9312	MS ES	AC	1990	LF9335	MS	AC
1941	LF8677		E	1991	LF9307	AS	S
1942	LF9315	MS	AC	1992	LF9305	AS	S
1943	LF9274	AS	A	1993	LF9306	AS*ke	S
1944	LF9266	AS*	J	1994	LF9304	AS	S
1945	LF9267	AS	AD	1995	LF9327	Ms	AC
1946	LF9284	AS	A	1996	LF8694	*	T
1947	LF8690		T	1997	LF8697	*	E
1948	LF9285	AS	AD	1998	LF9329	Ms	AC
1949	LF9281	AS	J	1999	LF9334	Ms	AC
1950	LF9282	AS	J	2000	LF8699		E

No.	Ref	Codes	Status	No.	Ref	Codes	Status
2001	LF9331	MS	AC	2051	LF9360	MS	AC
2002	LF9332	MS ME(r)	AC	2052	LF8714		
2003	LF9340	MS	AC	2053	LF9359	MS	AC
2004	LF8698	CS		2054	LF9363	MS	AC
2005	LF9328	MS	AC	2055	LF8717		AC
2006	LF8700		E	2056	LF8715	*ke-c	
2007	LF8701	*	E	2057	LF8716		N
2008	LF9330	MS	AC	2058	LF8719	*r9g	N
2009	LF8696		E	2059	LF9364	MS	AC
2010	LF9339	MS ME(r)	AC	2060	LF9981	L-d	AC
2011	LF8695	*	E	2061	LF9362	MS	AC
2012	LF9338	MS CS	AC	2062	LF8720	*ke	E
2013	LF9350	MS ME(r)	AC	2063	LF8721	*r9-ch(C3	P
2014	LF9336	MS	AC	2064	LF8726		B
2015	LF9337	MS	AC	2065	LF9367	MS	AC
2016	LF8704		E	2066	LF9368	MS	AC
2017	LF9344	MS ME(r)	AC	2067	LF8722	*	
2018	LF8705	* r5	E	2068	LF8725		AC
2019	LF9341	MS	AC	2069	LF8723	ES	
2020	LF8709	*re	AC	2070	LF8727	*L/177	
2021	LF8708		X	2071	LF8724	*rx	AC
2022	LF8702	*	X	2072	LE9414	L-d	
2023	LF9343	MS	AC	2073	LF8729	*ke	AC
2024	LF8703		X	2074	LF8728		AC
2025	LF9352	MS AE	AC	2075	LF8730	*	AC
2026	LF9345	MS	AC	2076	LF8732	*	AC
2027	LF9346	MS d-sx	AC	2077	LF8731	*r9	AC
2028	LF8710		AC	2078	LF8733		AC
2029	LF9342	MS AE	AC	2079	LF8734		AC
2030	LF9347	MS	AC	2080	LF8736	*ke	AC
2031	LF9348	MS ME(r)	AC	2081	LF8738		E
2032	LF8706	ME(r)	AC	2082	LF8735	*R9	
2033	LF8718	*		2083	LF8739	*	B
2034	LF8707			2084	LF8741		B
2035	LF8711	*re		2085	LF8737	*	E
2036	LE9407	L-d-sx		2086	LF9372	MS*ke	AC
2037	LE9406	L-ss-re ES		2087	LF8740	*	
2038	LF8712	*		2088	LF8746	*	A
20?9	LF8713	*		2089	LF8743	*	E
2040	LF9353	MS	AC	2090	LF8742	*ke-L	
2041	LF9349	MS	AC	2091	LF9369	MS	AC
2042	LF9364	MS	AC	2092	LF8745	*	F
2043	LF9361	MS	AC	2093	LF8744	*ke	Y
2044	LF9351	MS	AC	2094	LF8748	*	
2045	LF9366	MS	AC	2095	LF8749	*	T
2046	LF9365	MS	AC	2096	LF8750	r5 ME(r)	
2047	LF9356	MS	AC	2097	LF9387	MS	AC
2048	LF9357	MS	AC	2098	LF8752	*	AC
2049	LF9355	MS	AC	2099	LF8747	*	AC
2050	LF9358	MS	AC	2100	LF8754	*r5 ME(r)	AC

2101	LF8751	*	T	2151	LF9424	MS CS	AC
2102	LF8755	*re	AC	2152	LF9386	MS	AC
2103	LF8753	*		2153	LF9383	MS	AC
2104	LF8769	*		2154	LF8787	*	
2105	LF8762	*	AC	2155	LF9384	MS	AC
2106	LF8756		AC	2156	LF8788	*ke	
2107	LF8760	*L/159		2157	LF8792		
2108	LF8757	*	AC	2158	LF9390	MS	AC
2109	LF8758	*ke		2159	LF9391	MS	AC
2110	LF8759	*		2160	LF9392	MS	AC
2111	LF8766	*L/171		2161	LF8789	*	
2112	LF8763	*ke	A	2162	LF9396	MS	AC
2113	LF8765	*re		2163	LF9397	MS	AC
2114	LF8761			2164	LF9393	MS	AC
2115-	LF8771	*	AC	2165	LF8793		
2116	LF8764	*	T	2166	LF8790		
2117	LF8767	*	AC	2167	LF9395	MS	AC
2118	LF9371	MS*	AC	2168	LF8794		
2119	LF8768	*	AC	2169	LF9394	MS	AC
2120	LF9370	MS*	AC	2170	LF9421	MS CS	AC
2121	LF8770	*	A	2171	LF9398	MS	AC
2122	LF8773	*ke		2172	LF9399	MS NO	AC
2123	LF8775	d-c	AC	2173	LF8800	*	
2124	LF8772	CS	AC	2174	LF8801		
2125	LF8784	*		2175	LF8802	d-sx	
2126	LF8774	*ke ES		2176	LF9422	MS	AC
2127	LF8779	*	AC	2177	LF9423	MS	AC
2128	LF8778			2178	LF9425	MS	AC
2129	LF8776		AC	2179	LF8796		T
2130	LF9374	MS*ke	AC	2180	LF8795		
2131	LF8777		A	2181	LF8797	*ke	
2132	LF8780	*		2182	LF8811	*	
2133	LF8783	*re	T	2183	LF8827	*r6	A
2134	LF8781		A	2184	LF9426	MS	AC
2135	LF9375	MS*re	AC	2185	LF8798	*r5	
2136	LF9373	MS	AC	2186	LF8799		M
2137	LF8782	*		2187	LF9427	MS	AC
2138	LF9377	MS	AC	2188	LF8803		AC
2139	LF9379	MS	AC	2189	LF9428	MS	AC
2140	LF9385	MS	AC	2190	LF8804		AC
2141	LF9376	MS	AC	2191	LF8806		
2142	LF8785	*r9		2192	LF8817		AC
2143	LF9378	MS	AC	2193	LF9430	MS	AC
2144	LF9380	MS	AC	2194	LF8807	CS	
2145	LF8791			2195	LF9429	MS	AC
2146	LF9388	MS	AC	2196	LF8810		AE
2147	LF9339	MS	AC	2197	LF8812	*	
2148	LF9382	MS	AC	2198	LF8813		AC
2149	LF8786	*ke		2199	LF8809	*	AC
2150	LF9381	MS	AC	2200	LF8808	*	

2201	LF8805		AE	2251	LF8865	d-L	AE
2202	LF8820		AE	2252	LF8867		AE
2203	LF8822	*		2253	LF8862	AE.	B
2204	LF8815	*		2254	LF8877		AE
2205	LF8821		AC	2255	LF8868		AE
2206	LF8823	*		2256	LF8866		AE
2207	LF8824		P	2257	LF8871		AE
2208	LF8828	*	AE	2258	LF8870		AC
2209	LF8819			2259	LF8869		AE
2210	LF8830			2260	LF8878		AE
2211	LF8844		AE	2261	LF8874		AE
2212	LF8831		AE	2262	LF8875	*kE-L	
2213	LF8846		AE	2263	LF8876		AE
2214	LF8841		AE	2264	LF8873	*re- L-d	
2215	LF8816	ss-d-ke	C	2265	LF8880		AE
2216	LF8835	*L/184-d		2266	LF8899		AE
2217	LF8833		AE	2267	LF8881		AE
2213	LF8818	ss-d-ke	C	2268	LF8879		AE
2219	LF8814	ss-d-ke	C	2269	LF8902		AE
2220	LF8843	CS	AC	2270	LF8886	*	
2221	LF8832	ss	C	2271	LF9946	SN.	AB
2222	LF8826	ss-d-ke	C	2272	LF8882		AE
2223	LF8825	S	C	2273	LF8887		AE
2224	LF8829	ss	C	2274	LF8894		AE
2225	LF8838		AE	2275	LF9955	SN	AB
2226	LF8839		AC	2276	LF8884	ES	AE
2227	LF8840	d-sx NO	AE	2277	LF8883		AE
2228	LF8845	*ke	A	2278	LF8885		AE
2229	LF8842		AE	2279	LF8891		AE
2230	LF8854	ME(r)	AE	2280	LF8893		AE
2231	LF8855		AE	2281	LF8889		AE
2232	LF8852		AE	2282	LF8896		AE
2233	LF8849		AE	2283	LF8892		AP
2234	LF8850			2284	LF8888		AE
2235	LF8851		AE	2285	LF9951	SN	AB
2236	LF8848		AE	2286	LF9963	SN	AB
2237	LF8847		AE	2287	LF9952	SN	AB
2238	LF8857		AE	2288	LF9949	SN	AB
2239	LF8856		AE	2289	LF9947	SN	AB
2240	LF8853		AE	2290	LF9950	SN	AB
2241	LF8858		AE	2291	LF9954	SN	AB
2242	LF8837	ss-d-re	C	2292	LF8890		AE
2243	LF8836	ss-sx NO	C	2293	LF8900		AE
2244	LF8834	ss-d-ke	C	2294	LF9948	SN	AB
2245	LF8859		AE	2295	LF8903		AE
2246	LF8861		AE	2296	LN 296	L*	
2247	LF8864	* re	AE	2297	LF8898	CS	AE
2248	LF8872	* r5	AE	2298	LF8897		AE
2249	LF8860'	* r9 ES	AE	2299	LF9698	ME	AK
2250	LF8863	*	AE	2300	LF8895		AE

2301	LF8904		AE		2351	LF8944		
2302	LF9697	ME	AK		2352	LF8936		AL
2303	LF8901		AE		2353	LF8938	*ke	
2304	LF8906		AE		2354	LF9695	ME	AK
2305	LF9696	ME	AK		2355	LF8939	*ke	
2306	LF8912		AE		2356	LF8942		
2307	LF8907		AE		2357	LF8940	*ke	
2308	LF9687	ME	AK		2358	LF8943	*ke	AL
2309	LF8905		AE		2359	LF8945	*L/153	AL
2310	LF8909		AE		2360	LF8949	*	
2311	LF9700	ME	AK		2361	LF8948	*rx	
2312	LF8913		AE		2362	LF8947	*ke	
2313	LF8908	CS	AE		2363	LF8946	*ke	
2314	LF9705	ME	AK		2364	LF8950	*ke	
2315	LF8910	*ke			2365	LF8953	*ke	AE
2316	LF8918	* r5 ME(r)			2366	LF8954	*ke	
2317	LF9689	ME	AK		2367	LF8951	*re ES	AP
2318	LF8911	*ke			2368	LF8952	*ke	
2319	LF8917	CS			2369	LF8955	* r9 ES	AN
2320	LF9699	ME	AK		2370	LF8956	*ke	
2321	LF8914	*			2371	LF8958	*re	AP
2322	LF8915	*			2372	LF8959	*	
2323	LF9708	ME	AK		2373	LF8962	*ke	AP
2324	LF8919	*			2374	LF8957	*ke	
2325	LF8916	*	X		2375	LF8961	*ke	
2326	LF9686	ME	AK		2376	LF8964	*	
2327	LF8921	*re			2377	LF8960	*ke	AP
2328	LF8926	*r5			2378	LF8965	*	
(2329)	-	z			2379	LF8966	*	
2330	LF9692	ME	AK		2380	LF8963	*re	
2331	LF8922	CS			2381	LF8968	*r9	
2332	LF8924				2382	LF8967	*	
2333	LF9694	ME	AK		2383	LF8969	*ke	AP
2334	LF8920		X		2384	LF8973	*	AP
2335	LF8925		X		2385	LF8970	*re	
2336	LF9693	ME	AK		2386	LF8974	*	AP
2337	LF8923				2387	LF8971	*ke	
2338	LF8927	*			2388	LF8975	*L/156	
2339	LF9690	ME	AK		2339	LF8976	*r9	AP
2340	LF8934	CS			2390	LF8977	*r9	
2341	LF8931	*			2391	LF8972	*L/175	
2342	LF9691	ME	A K		2392	LF8979	*	AP
2343	LF8930	*ke			2393	LF8978	*ke	
2344	LF8929	*r5			2394	LF8980	*ke	G
2345	LF8937				2395	LF8981	*re ES	
2346	LF8928	*ke			2396	LF8982	*re	AP
2347	LF8933				2397	LF8983	*ke	AP
2348	LF8941		AN		2398	LF8986	*	AP
2349	LF8932	*r5			2399	LF8989	*r9	AP
2350	LF8935				2400	LF8991	*	AP

2401	LF8984	*r9		2451	LF9585	ME *r5	AK
2402	LF8987	*	AP	2452	LF8021	*re	AP
2403	LF8997	*L/152	AP	2453	LF9582	ME*	AK
2404	LF8998	*r9	AP	2454	LF9583	ME	AK
2405	LF8992	*r9	AP	2455	LH8024	*ke.	
2406	LF8995	*	AP	2456	LF9584	ME	AK
2407	LF8999	*ke	AP	2457	LH8022	*re	AP
2408	LF8990	*r9	M	2458	LH8025	*r6	
2409	LF8985	*re	Q	2459	LH8023	*	AP
2410	LF8996	*	AL	2460	LF9880	CN* ke	AH
2411	LF8988	*	AP	2461	LH8026	*	AP
2412	LF8993	*		2462	LF8028	*	
2413	LF9887	CN *ke	AH	2463	LH8052	*r6 ME(r)	
2414	LF9888	CN *re	AH	2464	LH8027	*	
2415	LH8001	*	AP	2465	LF9580	ME	AK
2416	LF9885	CN *ke	AH	2466	LH8029	*	A
2417	LF9884	CN*	AH	2467	LF9883	CN*	AH
2418	LF9886	CN*	AH	2468	LF9597	ME	AK
2419	LH8004	*ke	AP	2469	LF9589	ME *re	AK
2420	LF8994	*	H	2470	LF9882	CN *ke	AH
2421	LH8003	*ke	AP	2471	LH8031	*ke	AP
2422	LH8005	*		2472	LH8030	*ke-L/198	
2423	LH8002	*re		2473	LH8054	*ke	
2424	LH8006	*r6		2474	LF9587	*ME*	AK
2425	LH8007	*ke		2475	LH8034	*ke	AP
2426	LH8008	*ke		2476	LF9586	ME	AK
2427	LH8012	*		2477	LF9881	CN *rg	AH
2428	LH8009	*		2478	LH8036	*L/172	
2429	LH8015	*r 9 ES		2479	LF9588	ME	AK
2430	LH8011	*		2480	LF8647	L/159	
2431	LH8010	*L/162	AP	2481	LH8117	L* r9	
2432	LH8013	*ke		2482	LF9590	ME	AK
2433	LH8016	*re	AP	2483	LH8032	*ke	AP
2434	LH8017	*ke	AP	2484	LH8033	*ke	A
2435	LH8020	*re	AP	2485	LF9591	ME*r6	AK
2436	LH8019	L*	AP	2486	LH8037	*	M
2437	LF9704	ME	AK	2487	LH8038	*re	AF
2438	LH8018	*		2488	LH8053	*ke-L/195	AP
2439	LF9688	ME	AK	2489	LF9594	ME*	AK
2440	LF9710	ME	AK	2490	LF9889	CN*	AH
2441	LH8014	* ke	AP	2491	LF9648	ME *ke	AK
2442	LF9706	ME	AK	2492	LF9890	CN *r9	AH
2443	LF9685	ME AE	AK	2493	LF9593	ME*	AK
2444	LF9702	ME	AK	2494	LH8035	*r9	
2445	LF9701	ME	AK	2495	LF9592	ME*	AK
2446	LF9713	ME	AK	2496	LH8041	*ke	A
2447	LF9707	ME	AK	2497	LH8044	*	AF
2448	LF9709	ME	AK	2498	LF9595	ME*r6	AK
2449	LF9703	ME CS	AK	2499	LH8039	ke	AP
2450	LF9581	ME	AK	2500	LH8059	*	AP

2501	LF9463	ME *ke	AK	2551	LF9675	ME	N
2502	LH8040	*ke	AP	2552	LH8077	*	AP
2503	LH8084	*rx	AP	2553	LH8080	* r6 ME (r)	AP
2504	LF9644	ME*	AK	2554	LF9674	ME	N
2505	LH8055	*	AP	2555	LH8128	d-L/61 ke	
2506	LF9642	ME	AK	2556	LH8048	* re	AF
2507	LH8051	*ke	AP	2557	LF9677	ME	AK
2508	LH8064	*	AP	2558	LH8087	*r9	AP
2509	LF9645	ME	N	2559	LF9682	ME	N
2510	LH8042	*re	AF	2560	LH8049	*ke	AF
2511	LH8057	*	AP	2561	LH8081	* ke	AF
2512	LF9647	ME	N	2562	LF8083	*	AP
2513	LH8043	* r9	A	2563	LF9684	ME	AK
2514	LF9891	CN*	AH	2564	LH8082	*	AP
2515	LF9646	ME	N	2565	LH8086	*r6 ME(r)	AP
2516	LH8063	*	AP	2566	LF9683	ME	AK
2517	LH8056	*ke	AP	2567	no.reg.	c	
2518	LF9640	ME	AK	2568	LH8085	*	AP
2519	LH8062	*ke	AP	2569	LF9681	ME	AK
2520	LH8058	*ke	AP	2570	LN 238	L- ss	
2521	LF9641	ME	AK	2571	LH8050	*ke	A
2522	LH8060	*	AP	2572	LH8097	*	AP
2523	LH8061	*ke	M	2573	LF9716	ME	AK
2524	LF9639	ME*	AK	2574	LH8098	*	AF
2525	LH8065	*r6		2575	LH8088	*	AP
2526	LH8045	*re		2576	LF9711	ME	AK
2527	LH8073	*	G	2577	LH8092	*re	AE
2528	LF9638	ME	N	2578	LF9784	ME	AK
2529	LH8067	*ke	G	2579	LF9719	ME	AK
2530	LN 298	L-ss-d-re		2580	LH8095	*	AP
2531	LF9637	ME	AK	2581	LH8090	*ke	B
2532	LH8046	*re	AF	2582	LH8091	*	AP
2533.	LH8070	*re	AP	2583	LF9718	ME	AK
2634	LF9679	ME	AK	2584	LH8099	*ke	AP
2535	LH8068	*ke	G	2585	LF9721	ME	AK
2636	LH8071	*	G	2586	LH8094	*ke	M
2537	LH8066	*	G	2587	LH8108	*	X
2538	LF9678	ME	N	(2588)		z	
2539	LH8069.	* r9	G	2589	LF9712	ME	AK
2540	LF9680	ME	N	7590	LH8096	*r5	M
2641	LH8047	*	AF	2591	LF9714	ME	AK
2542	LH8072	*	G	2592	LH8101	* ke	M
2643	LF9635	ME	N	2593	LF9717	ME	AK
2544	LH8075	*		2594	LF9774	ME	AF
2545	LH8076	*G		2595	LH8106	*	AL
2546	LF9636	ME	N	2596	LF9775	ME	AF
2547	LH8078	* r9		2597	LF9720	ME	AK
2548	LF9076	ME	AK	2598	LH8104	* re	AE
2549	LH8079	*re	AP	(2599)		z	
2550	LH8074	*rx	AP	(2600)		z	

2601	LH8103	*	AL	2651	LH8122	*r9	X
2602	LF9776	ME	AF	2652	LH8110	*ke	X
2603	LH8107	* re	AF	2653	LF9798	ME	AF
2604	LF9722	ME	AK	2654	LF9730	ME	AK
2605	LH8105	* ke	B	2655	LF9727	ME	AK
2606	LF9777	ME	AF	2656	LH8125	*ke	
2607	LF9723	ME	AK	2657	LH8114	*r9	
2608	LF9778	ME	AF	2658	LH8119	*ke	
2609	LF9736	ME	AK	2659	LH8124	*ke-L/191	
2610	LF9779	ME	AF	2660	LH8314	* r6 ME(r)	
2611	LH8118	*	X	2661	LH8100	*ke	X
2612	LF9739	ME	AK	2662	LH8123	*ke	B
2613	LF9733	ME	AK	2663	LH8120	*re	X
2614	LN215	L-d ME(r)		(2664)	AH0187	z	
2615	LF9738	ME	AK	2665	LH8126	*re	X
2616	LF9780	ME	AF	2666	LH8121	*	X
2617	LF9715	ME	AK	2667	LH8111	*L/1 66	
2618	LF9781	ME	AF	2668	LH8102	*ke	X
2619	LF9737	ME	AK	2669	LF9726	ME	AK
2620	LF9732	ME	AK	2670	LF9728	ME	AK
2621	LF9735	ME	AK	2671	LH8113	*re	X
2622	LC2823	L-d ME (r)		2672	LH8112	*ke	
(2623)	AH0138	z		(2673)	AH0189	z	
2624	LF9734	ME	AK	2674	LH8089	*re	
2625	LF9724	ME	AK	2675	LH8109	sb *ke	X
2626	LF9740	ME	AK	2676	LH8116	*	
2627	LF9741	ME	AK	2677	LH8199		
(2628	AH0139	z		2678	LH8127		
2629	LF9785	ME	AF	2679	LH8093	st*	
2630	LF9742	M E	AK	2680	LH8129	st*	C
2631	LF9786	M E	AF	2681	LH8130	st*	C
2632	LF9782	M E	AF	2682	LH8131	st*	C
2633	LF9725	M E	AK	2683	LH8132	st*	C
2634	LF9787	M E	AF	2684	LH8133	st*	C
2635	LF9729	M E	AK	2685	LH8134	st*	C
2636	LF9788	M E	AF	2686	LH8135	st*	C
2637	LF9783	M E	AF	2687	LH3136	st*re	C
2638	LF9790	M E	AF	2688	LH8137	st*	C
(2639)	AH0140	z		2689	LH8138	st*	AN
(2640)		z		2690	LH8139	st*	AN
2641	LF9791	ME	AF	2691	LH8140	st*	AN
2642	LF9797	ME	AF	2692	LH8141	st*	AN
2643	LF9792	ME	AF	2693	LH8142	st*re	AH
2644	LF9793	ME	AF	2694	LH8143	st*	AH
2645	LF9794	ME	AF	2695	LH8144	st*	AH
2646	LF9789	ME	AF	2696	LH8145	st*	AH
2647	LF9795	ME	AF	2697	LH8146	st*	J
2648	LF9796	ME	AF	2698	LH8147	st*	J
2649	LH8115	*ke	X	2699	LH8148	st*	J
(2650)	AH0141	z		2700	LH8149	st*	J

2701	LH8150	st *re	J	2751	LH8716	z	
2702	LH8151	st *	J	2752	LH8202	*ke	
2703	LH8152	st *	J	2753	LH8203	*ke	
2704	LH8153	st *L/170	J	2754	LH8204	*r9	
2705	LH8154	st *re	J	2755	LH8205	*r9	
2706	LH8155	st*	J	2756	LH8206	*	
2707	LH8156	st*	AN	2757	LH8207	*	
2708	LH8157	st8	AN	2758	LH8208	*ke-L	
2709	LH8158	*r9	M	2759	LH8209	*re	
2710	LH8159	*L/1 55	M	2760	LH8210	*	
2711	LH8160	*r9	M	2761	LH8211	*	
2712	LH8161	*re	M	2762	LH8212	*	
2713	LH8162	*ke-L/194-d	ESM	2763	LH8213	*	
2714	LH8163	*re	M	2764	LH8214	*ke-ch	
2715	LH8164	*re	M	2765	LH8215	*ke	
2716	LH8165	*re	M	2766	LH8216	*k	
2717	LH8166	*	M	2767	LH8217	*	
2718	LH8187	*r9	M	2768	LH8218	*ke	
2719	LH8168	*re	M	2769	LH8219	*ke ES	
2720	LH8169	*r6ME(r)	M	2770	LH8220	*	
2721	LH8170	*ke	M	2771	LH8221	*ke	
2722	LH8171	*	M	2772	LH8222	*	
2723	LH8172	*rx	M	2773	LH8223	*r9	
2724	LH8173	*ke	M	2774	LH8224	*	
2725	LH8174	*r9	M	2775	LH8275	*ke	
2726	LH8175	*L/167	M	2776	LH8226	*re	
2727	LH8176	*r9	M	2777	LH8227	*	
2728	LH8177	*ke	M	2778	LH8228	*	
2729	LH8179	* re	M	2779	LH8229	*	
2730	LH8179	*r6ME(r)	M	2780	LH8230	*ke	
2731	LH8180	*L/*165	M	2781	LH8231	*ke	
2732	LH8181	*ke	M	2782	LH8232	*r9	
2733	LH8182	*r6ME(r)	M	2783	LH8233	*L/1 85	
2734	LH8183	*ke	M	2784	LH8234	*ke	
2735	LH8184	*r6 *ME(r)	M	2785	LH8235	*c	
2736	LH8185	*ke	M	2786	LH8236	*ke	
2737	LH8186	*ke	M	2787	LH8237	*	
2738	LH8167	*re	M	2788	LH8238	*ke	
2739	LH8188	*	M	2789	LH8239	*r9	
2740	LH8189	*		2790	LH8240	*	
2741	LH8190	*ke		2791	LH8241	*r9 ES	
2742	LH8191	*r6 *ME(r)		2792	LH8242	*ke	
2743	LH8192	*r6 *ME(r)		2793	LH8243	*	
2744	LH8193	*ke		2794	LH8244	*ke	
2745	LH8194	*re-L-d		2795	LH8245	*ke	
2746	LH8195	*r9		2796	LH8246	*	
2747	LH8196	*ke		2797	LH8247	*re	
2748	LH8197	*re		2798	LH8248	*ke ES	
2749	LH8198	*r9		2799	LH8249	*ke	
2750	LH8200	* re		2800	LH8250	r*e	

2801	LH8251	*r6 *ME(r)		3479	LH8280	st	C
2802	LH8252	*re		3480	LH8282	st	J
2803	LH8253	*ke		3481	LH8286	st	J
2804	LH8254	*rx		3482	LH8284	st	C
2805	LH8255	*ke		3483	LH8283	st	C
2806	LH8256	*r9		3884	LH8287	st	C
2807	LH8257	*re-st		3485	LH8288	st	C
2808	LH8258	*ke		3486	LH8293	st	C
2809	LH8259	*ke		3487	LH8294	st	C
2810	LH8260	*r9		3488	LH8295	st	C
2811	LH8261	*ke		3489	LH8296	st	C
2812	LH8262	*ke		3490	LH8300	st	AK
2813	LH8263	*r9		3491	LH8297	st	C
2815	LH8265	*ke		3492	LH8298	st	AK
2816	LH8266	*ke		3493	LH8301	st	AK
2817	LH8267	*		3494	LF8299	st	AK
2819	LH8269	*re		3495	LH8302	st	C
2821	LH8271	*r9		3496	LH8306	st	AK
2822	LH8272	*L/1*61		3497	LH8307	st	AK
2825	LH8275	*		3498	LF8308	st	AK
2826	LH8315			3499	LH8303	st	AK
2830	LH8289	ch		3500	LH8304	st	AK
2832	LH8290	ch		3501	LH8305	st	AK
2834	LH8291	ch		3502	LH8309	st	AB
2836	LF8292	ch		3503	LH8310	st	C
2838	LC3761	L					
2841	LC3759	L		3706	LC8678	L*r5 ME (r)	
2850	LH8348	L-d-st-- ke		3710	LH8201		
2851	LH8349	L-d-st - ke		3732	LC2245	L*r5 ME(r)	
2852	LH8350	L-d-st - ke		3744	LH8341	L*r6 ME(r)	
2853	LH8351	L-d		3758	LN 202	L*r6 ME(rk	
2854	LH8352	L-st		3769	LC5080	L*r5 ME(r)	
2855	LH8353	L-d-st -ke.		3772	LH8264	L*r5	
2856	LH8354	L		3805	LH8268		
2857	LH8355	L-d-st-ke		3806	LH8276		
2858	LH8356	L-d-st -ke		3813	LH8270		
2859	LH8357	L-d-st		3814	LP8683	ME(r)	
				3815	LH8273		
3163	LH8905	ch *-		3816	LH8274		
3164	LH8906	ch *-					
3165	LB8907	ch *-		4865	LH8342	L	
3166	LE8908	ch *-		4866	LH8343	L-d-st-ke	
3167	LH8909	ch *-		4867	LH8344	L	
3168	LH8910	ch *-		4868	LH8345	L-d-ke	
				4869	LH8358	ss-d-re	
3474	LH8277	st	C	4870	LH8359	ss-st	
3475	LH8278	st	C	4871	LH8360	ss-d-re	
3476	LH8279	st	C	4872	LH8361	ss-d-re	
3477	LH8285	st	C	4873	LH8362	ss-d-re	
3478	LH8281	st	C	4874	LH8363	ss-d-ke	

4875	LH8364	ss-d-re	4925	LH8482	d-sx
4876	LH8365	ss	4926	LH8416	
4877	LH8366	ss	4927	LH8390	M E (r)
4878	LH8367	ss	4928	LH8565	d-sx-st
4879	LH8368		4929	LH8563	
4880	LH8369	L	4930	LH8412	NO
4881	LH8370	L	4931	LH8393	NO
4882	LH8371	L	4932	LH8439	CS
4883	LH8372		4933	LH8391	d-sx
4884	LH8374	ME (r)	4934	LH8550	d-sx NO
4885	LH8375	NO	4935	LH8406	
4886	LH8376		4936	LH8408	
4887	LH8373	ME (r)	4937	LH8414	NO
4888	LH8377	ME(r)	4938	LH8410	NO
4889	LH8378	ME (r)	4939	LH8570	
4890	LH8379	ME (r)	4940	LH8438	
4891	LH8380		4941	LH8426	
4892	LH8381	ME(r)	4942	LH8486	
4893	LH8384		4943	LH8522	
4894	LH8382		4944	LH8405	
4895	LH8386		4945	LH8422	
4896	LH8400	NO	4946	LH8564	d-sx
4897	LH8392	ME(r)	4947	LH8548	
4898	LH8389	AE	4948	LH8435	
4899	LH8402		4949	LH8411	
4900	LH8385	d-sx	4950	LH8547	d-sx
4901	LH8388	d-sx NO	4951	LH8545	d sx NO
4902	LH8403	NO	4952	LH8533	d-sx
4903	LH8383	AE	4953	LH8464	d-sx
4904	LH8387	d-sx NO	4954	LH8434	
4905	LH8407	d-sx	4955	LH8429	
4906	LH8394		4956	LH8420	
4907	LH8399		4957	LH8436	
4908	LH8430		4958	LH8569	d-sx
4909	LH8432		4959	LH8421	
4910	LH8561		4960	LH8425	NO
4911	LH8413		4961	LH8424	
4912	LH8423		4962	LH8419	
4913	LH8415		4963	LH8418	
4914	LH8396		4964	LH8546	d-sx NO
4915	LH8404		4965	LH8427	
4916	LH8560		4966	LH8555	d-sx
4917	LH8401	NO	4967	LH8440	
4918	LH8441		4968	LH8538	d-sx-st
4919	LH8431	AE	4969	LH8523	d-sx-st
4920	LH8397	NO	4970	LH8585	
4921	LH8433		4971	LH8437	
4922	LH8395		4972	LH8417	
4923	LH8409		4973	LH8525	d-sx
4924	LH8398	NO	4974	LH8543	d-sx NO

4975	LH8469	d-sx		5025	LH8554	d-sx-d NO
4976	LH8528			5026	LU8008	
4977	LH8463	d-sx		5027	LH8521	d-sx-d NO
4978	LH8566	d-sx		5028	LH8465	
4979	LH8483			5029	LU8017	
4980	LH8572			5030	LH8591	
4981	LH8568			5031	LU8015	
4982	LH8552	d-sx NO		5032	LH8600	d-sx
4983	LH8481			5033	LH8470	
4984	LH8484			5034	LH8593	
4985	LH8541	d-sx		5035	LH8598	
4986	LH8487	d-sx		5036	LH8559	d-sx
4987	LH8524			5037	LH8558	NO
4988	LH8472	d-sx		5038	LH8448	
4989	LH8476	d-Sx		5039	LH8446	
4990	LH8471			5040	LU8013	
4991	LU8020	AE		5041	LU8009	
4992	LU8016	NO		5042	LH8467	
4993	LH8428	AE		5043	LH8468	d-L
4994	LH8532	d-sx-st		5044	LH8551	d-sx-d
4995	LH8596			5045	LH8553	d-sx
4996	LH8535			5046	LH8466	
4997	LU8018			5047	LH8556	d-sx
4998	LH8473	d-sx		5048	LH8460	
4999	LH8474	d-sx NO		5049	LH8462	
5000	LU8004			5050	LH8458	
5001	LH8595			5051	LH8455	
5002	LU8007			5052	LH8450	AE
5003	LU8023			5053	LH8451	
5004	LU8021			5054	LH8459	d-sx
5005	LU8025	AE		5055	LH8454	CS
5006	LU8006			5056	LH8457	
5007	LU8012			5057	LH8449	
5008	LH8557	d-sx		5058	LH8461	
5009	LU8014			5059	LH8452	CS
5010	LH8599			5060	LH8456	
5011	LU8010	AE		5061	LH8453	
5012	LU8003	CS		5062	LH8497	d-sx
5013	LU8001	NO		5063	LH8500	
5014	LH8594			5064	LH8498	CS
5015	LU8011			5065	LH8488	d-sx
5016	LH8597			5066	LH8495	
5017	LU8024			5067	LH8503	d-sx
5018	LU8019			5068	LH8475	CS
5019	LU8002			5069	LH8512	d-sx
5020	LH8549	d-sx -d		5070	LH8494	
5021	LU8022			5071	LH8502	
5022	LU8005			5072	LH8499	NO
5023	LH8592			5073	LH8508	
5024	LH8447			5074	LH8573	

5075	LH8580	d-sx		5118	LH8501	
5076	LH8574			5119	LH8491	d-sx
5077	LH8576			5120	LH8496	d-sx
5078	LH8579	d-sx-d		5121	LH8540	d-sx
5079	LH8578	d-sx		5122	LH8513	
5080	LH8531	d-sx-st		5123	LH8536	d-sx-st
5081	LH8575	d-sx-d		5124	LH8537	d-sx
5082	LH8571			5125	LH8542	
5083	LH8479			5126	LH8582	d-sx
5084	LH8577	d-sx-d		5127	LH8567	d-sx
5085	LH8583	d-sx		5128	LH8586	
5086	LH8584			5129	LH8526	d-sx
5087	LH8480			5130	LH8562	d-sx
5088	LH8589	AE		5131	LH8581	
5089	LH8588			5132	LH8527	d-sx-st
5090	LH8478	d-sx NO		5133	LN4598	L(X39 rebuilt)
5091	LH8590			5134	LN9966	L(X58 rebuilt)
5092	LH8516	d-sx				
5093	LH8507			6865	LH8316	ME (r)
5094	LH8515			6866	LH8317	ME (r)
5095	LH8510	d-sxNO		6867	LH8318	ME (r)
5096	LH8477			6868	LH8319	ME (r)
5097	LH8534	d-sx-st		6869	LH8320	ME (*r) d L
5098	LH8587			6870	LH8321	ME (r)
5099	LH8504	d-sx NO		6871	LH8322	ME (r)
5100	LH8489			6872	LH8324	ME (r)
5101	LH8519			6873	LH8331	GL
5102	LH8514			6874	LH8330	ME (r)
5103	LH8518	d-sx-st		6875	LH8332	GL
5104	LH8517	d-sx		6876	LH8323	ME(r)
5105	LH8505	d-sx		6877	LH8333	GL
5106	LH8509	d-sx		6878	LH8325	ME(r)
5107	LH8539	d-sx		6879	LH8334	GL
5108	LH8520			6880	LH8335	GL
5109	LH8492	d-sx		6881	LH8336	GL
5110	LH8530	AE		6882	LH8326	ME(r)
5111	LH8493			6883	LH8337	GL
5112	LH8544	d-sx		6884	LH8338	GL
5113	LH8490			6885	LH8339	GL
5114	LH8485			6886	LH8327	ME (r)
5115	LH8511	d-sx		6881	LH8340	GL AE
5116	LH8506			6888	LH8328	ME(r)
5117	LH8529			6889	LH8329	ME(r)

APPENDIX B

GARAGE CODES REFFERRED TO IN THIS BOOK

A	ALBANY ST (to 1916)	W	CRICKLEW00D
	SUTTON (from 1924)	X	MIDDLE ROW
B	BATTERSEA	Y	CLAY HALL
C	ATHOL STREET	AB	TWICKENHAM
D	DALSTON	AC	WILLESDEN
E	ACTON (TO 1925)	AD	PALMERS GREEN
F	FULHAM (FARM LANE)	AE	HENDON
	(to 1914)	AF	PUTNEY
	PUTNEY BRIDGE*		(CHELVERTON ROAD)
	(from 1920)		
G	FOREST GATE	AH	KINGSTON (to 1914)
H	HACKNEY		NUNHEAD* (from 1920
J	HOLLOWAY	AJ	COLINDALE
K	KILBURN (to 1914)	AK	STREATHAM
	KINGSTON (from 1922)	AL	MERTON
L	LOUGHTON	AM	PLUMSTEAD
M	MORTLAKE	AN	CATFORD
N	NORWOOD	AP	SEVEN KINGS
P	OLD KENT ROAD	AR	TOTTENHAM
Q	PUTNEY (FELSHAM ROAD)	AV	HOUNSLOW
	(to 1913)		
	CAMBERWELL (from (1914)	BK	BARKING
R	FULHAM (NORMAND ROAD)	CF	CHALK FARM
	(to 1913)		
	HAMMERSMITH (from 1913)	HW	HANWELL
S	SHEPHERDS BUSH	RD	ROMFORD
T	LEYTON	SP	SIDCUP
U	UPTON PARK	WT	WATFORD
V	TURNHAM GREEN		

*taken over from National Steam Car Co Ltd.

APPENDIX   C

BUS ROUTES REFFERED TO IN THIS BOOK

1 Tower Bridge - Kilburn Station
2 Golders Green - Ebury Bridge
3 Camden Town - Crystal Palace
4 Finsbury Park - Bermondsey
5 Putney Hill - Stroud Green
6 Kensal Rise - South Hackney
7 Liverpool Street - Wormwood Scrubbs
8 Willesden - Seven Kings
8 Willesden - Old Ford (a)
9 Liverpool Street - Barnes
10A Elephant & Castle - Buckhurst Hill
11 Liverpool Street - Shepherds Bush
12 Turnham Green - Nunhead
13 London Bridge - Hendon
14 Putney - Hornsey Rise
14A Putney - Stroud Green
15 Putney - East Ham
16 Cricklewood - Victoria Station
17 Ealing - London Bridge Station
18 Willesden - London Bridge Station
19 Clapham Junction - Highbury Barn
20 Shepherd Bush - West Norwood
21 Wood Green - Deptford
22 Putney - Homerton
23 Acton Vale - Barking
24 Hampstead Heath - Pimlico
25 Victoria - Old Ford
25 Victoris - Seven Kings (a)
25A Victoria - Chadwell Heath
26 Kensal Rise - Hackney Wick
27 Twickenham - Highgate
28 Golders Green - Wandsworth Bridge
29 Victoria - Southgate
30 Putney - Highbury Station
31 Chelsea - Swiss Cottage

33 Charing Cross - Richmond
35 Elephant & Castle - Walthamstow
36 West Kilburn - Catford
37 Herne Hill - Isleworth
41 Muswell Hill - Crouch End
42 Finsbury Park - Camberwell Green
43 Muswell Hill - London Bridge
43A Colney Hatch Lane - London Bridge
45 Staines - Harlington (b)
48 Paddington Green - Blackheath
49 Shepherd Bush - Streatham Common
51A West Kilburn - Barking
56 Mile End Station - Millwall Docks
59 Camden Town - South Croydon
62 Hounslow - Windsor Castle (c)
63 Chalk Farm - Honor Oak
67A Stoke Newington - Wandsworth Com
68 South Hampstead - Tulse Hill
69 Poplar - Plumstead
71 Ealing - Surbiton
73 Barnes - Kings Cross
78 Shoreditch - Dulwich
79 Kingston - Esher
82 Hounslow - Staines
84 Golders Green - St Albans
85 Putney Bridge - Kingston
97 Ealing - Northfields
105 Ealing - Surbiton
106 Finsbury Park - Blackwell Tunnel
108 Bow - Blackheath
109 Penge - Woolwich
109 Penge - Chislehurst (d)
111 Finsbury Park - Muswell Hill
142 Kilburn - Watford
155 Golders Green - Hatfield

(a) Route changed 20/6/12

(b) Became 82 1/8/12
(c) Became 81 1/8/12
(d) Route after 1919